Workbook

Virginia Evans - Jenny Dooley

Express Publishing

Contents

STARTER UNIT Let's start .... p. 4

UNIT 1 1a Friends on the Net .... p. 6
        1b The world over .... p. 7
        1c Pleased to meet you! .... p. 8
        1d Writing .... p. 9
            Grammar in Use .... p. 10
            Reader's Corner .... p. 12
            Progress Check .... p. 13

UNIT 2 2a Family ties .... p. 14
        2b Families of the world .... p. 15
        2c Family fun! .... p. 16
        2d Writing .... p. 17
            Grammar in Use .... p. 18
            Reader's Corner .... p. 20
            Progress Check .... p. 21

UNIT 3 3a Day by day .... p. 22
        3b School days .... p. 23
        3c Careers day .... p. 24
        3d Writing .... p. 25
            Grammar in Use .... p. 26
            Reader's Corner .... p. 28
            Progress Check .... p. 29

UNIT 4 4a Fit for a Queen! .... p. 30
        4b Home exchange .... p. 31
        4c A new neighbourhood .... p. 32
        4d Writing .... p. 33
            Grammar in Use .... p. 34
            Reader's Corner .... p. 36
            Progress Check .... p. 37

UNIT 5 5a A matter of taste .... p. 38
        5b What's on the list? .... p. 39
        5c What's cooking? .... p. 40
        5d Writing .... p. 41
            Grammar in Use .... p. 42
            Reader's Corner .... p. 44
            Progress Check .... p. 45

UNIT 6 6a Weather blues .... p. 46
        6b In action! .... p. 47
        6c Just my style! .... p. 48
        6d Writing .... p. 49

            Grammar in Use .... p. 50
            Reader's Corner .... p. 52
            Progress Check .... p. 53

UNIT 7 7a Charmed lives! .... p. 54
        7b The way it was! .... p. 55
        7c It's all in the past! .... p. 56
        7d Writing .... p. 57
            Grammar in Use .... p. 58
            Reader's Corner .... p. 60
            Progress Check .... p. 61

UNIT 8 8a Once on Planet Earth … .... p. 62
        8b Animal hall of fame .... p. 63
        8c Storyline .... p. 64
        8d Writing .... p. 65
            Grammar in Use .... p. 66
            Reader's Corner .... p. 68
            Progress Check .... p. 69

UNIT 9 9a Tomorrow's world .... p. 70
        9b Action-packed! .... p. 71
        9c Making plans .... p. 72
        9d Writing .... p. 73
            Grammar in Use .... p. 74
            Reader's Corner .... p. 76
            Progress Check .... p. 77

UNIT 10 10a On your travels .... p. 78
        10b Well-travelled! .... p. 79
        10c Time for a change! .... p. 80
        10d Writing .... p. 81
            Grammar in Use .... p. 82
            Reader's Corner .... p. 84
            Progress Check .... p. 85

        Irregular Verbs .... p. 86

Let's Start

1 Crack the Code! Look and write.

B	C	D	E	F	G	H	I	J	K	L	M	N	O	P	Q	R	S	T	U	V	W	X	Y	Z	A
A	B	C	D	E	F	G	H	I	J	K	L	M	N	O	P	Q	R	S	T	U	V	W	X	Y	Z

IFMMP, XIBU'T ZPVS OBNF?

H..
....

Now, answer the question in code: ....

2 Teen Talk! Match the text messages to the sentences.

1 Do U 1t me 2 w8 4 U?   a That's great news!
2 How R U 2day?   b See you at seven!
3 That's gr8 news!   c Do you want me to wait for you?
4 CU @ 7!   d Okay for tomorrow.
5 OK 4 2morrow.   e How are you today?

3 Find and circle the colours. Then, write.

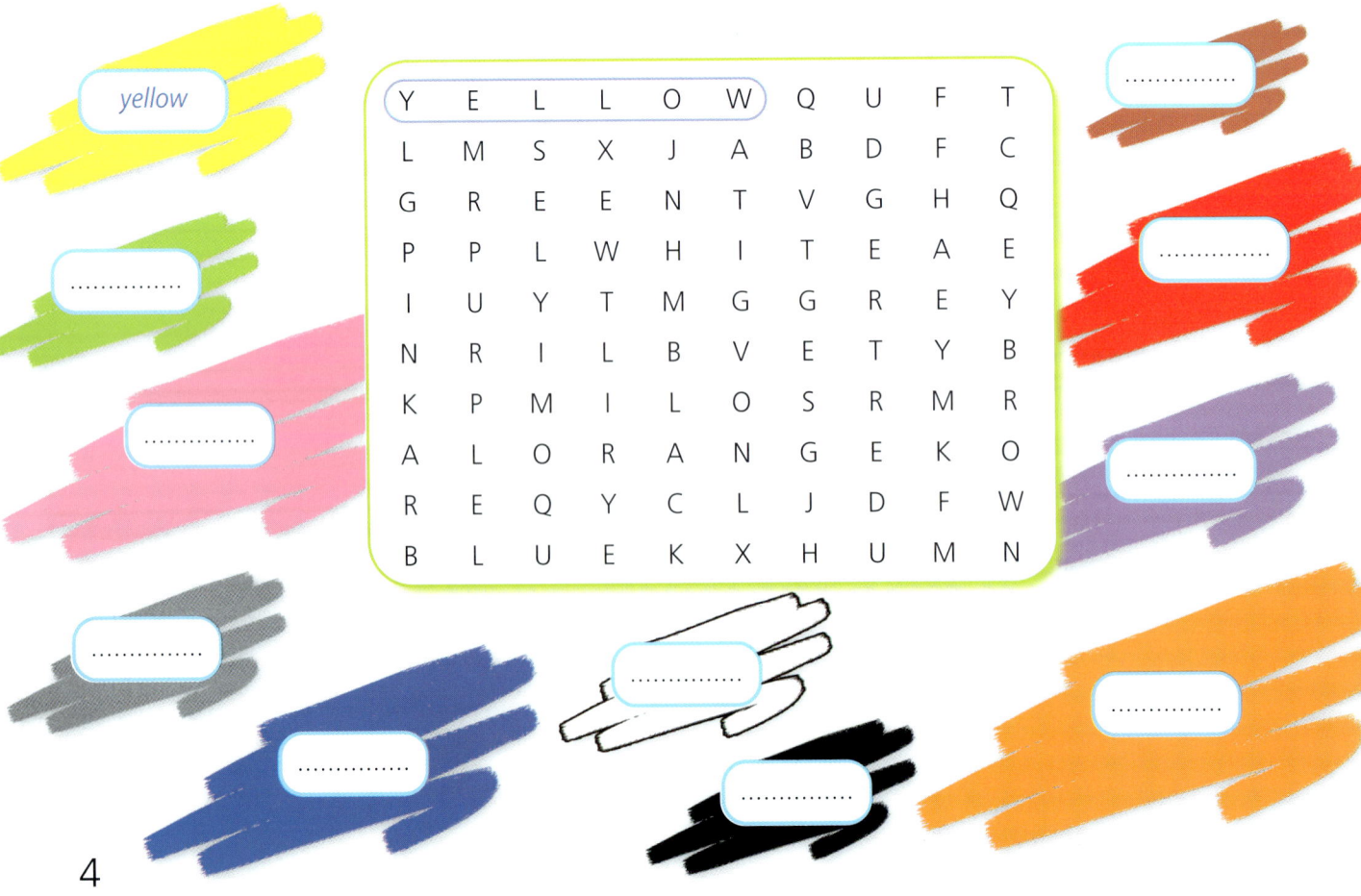

yellow

Y	E	L	L	O	W	Q	U	F	T
L	M	S	X	J	A	B	D	F	C
G	R	E	E	N	T	V	G	H	Q
P	P	L	W	H	I	T	E	A	E
I	U	Y	T	M	G	G	R	E	Y
N	R	I	L	B	V	E	T	Y	B
K	P	M	I	L	O	S	R	M	R
A	L	O	R	A	N	G	E	K	O
R	E	Q	Y	C	L	J	D	F	W
B	L	U	E	K	X	H	U	M	N

4

4 What are they? Look and write.

1 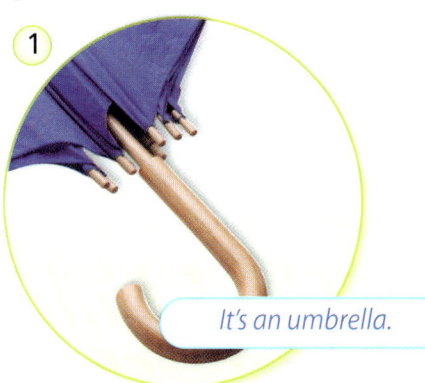 *It's an umbrella.*

2  ....

3  ....

4  ....

5  ....

6  ....

5 Fill in: *this*, *that*, *these*, *those*.

1   *This* is a cassette.

2   .... is a computer.

3   .... are dictionaries.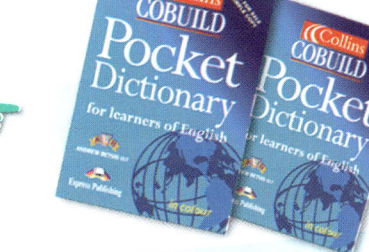

4   .... are sandwiches.

5   .... is a taxi.

6   .... is a bag.

5

1a Friends on the Net

Vocabulary Practice

1 Which country is it? Read and write.

		Country	
1	🇷🇺	*Russia*	.ru
2	🇵🇱	....	.pl
3	🇯🇵	....	.jp
4	🇬🇷	....	.gr
5	🇲🇽	....	.mx
6	🇹🇷	....	.tr

2 Where are they from? Look at their e-mail addresses and write.

e - Friends Photo Centre

1 nick-smith@msn.us
2 consuelo-ramirez@prodigy.net.mx
3 omar-hussein@tedata.eg
4 anna-pappa@forthnet.gr
5 richard-green@msn.co.uk
6 laila-jem@kablonet.tr

1 *He's from the USA.*
2 ....
3 ....
4 ....
5 ....
6 ....

Speaking

3 Talk with your partner.

1 A: What's your new e-friend's name?
B: Nick Smith.
A: Where's he from?
B: The USA.

The world over 1b

Vocabulary Practice

1 Write the nationalities in the correct column. Use your dictionaries, if necessary.

- Austria
- Germany
- Britain
- Spain
- USA
- Brazil
- Italy
- China
- Mexico
- Turkey
- Japan
- Russia
- Poland
- Egypt

-(i)an	-ish	-ese
Austrian	Spanish	....
....	....	....
....	....	....
....	....	....
....	....	....
....	....	....
....	....	....

2 a. Travel Quiz! Match the airlines to the countries. Then, say.

Delta Airlines
Aeroflot
Olympic Airways
EasyJet
Volare Airlines
Lufthansa
Iberia Airlines

Italy
Greece
USA
Britain
Russia
Spain
Germany

Delta Airlines is an American airline.

b. Do you know any other airlines? Tell the class.

Listening

3 🎧 Listen and choose.

1 Aniela and Dario are in
A a school canteen. B a classroom.

2 Aniela's surname is
A Waleska. B Sikorski.

3 Dario is
A 23. B 32.

4 Dario is from
A Spain. B Italy.

5 Aniela is
A French. B Polish.

Reading

4 Where are they? Look, read and fill in the country.

Here I am in London! It's a great city. I love 1) ....

Paris is a fantastic place. 2) .... is a great country!

I'm in Moscow now. It's very cold here, but I like 3) .... a lot!

7

1c Pleased to meet you!

Everyday English

1 a. Look, read and match.

1 Dad, this is Pat. ....
2 Goodbye, Daddy. ....
3 Lorraine, this is Mr Hills. ....
4 Hi, girls! How are things? ....

b. **Portfolio:** In pairs, decide what the other speaker is saying above. Act out short dialogues for each situation and record them.

Speaking

2 **Student A:** You are a famous person (e.g. actor, footballer). Write your personal information. Write: *name*, *age*, *country*, *nationality*, *favourite things* (*singer, colour, food etc.*).

Student B: Ask the following questions and keep notes:

• name? spell it? age? • where from?
• nationality? • favourite things?

Writing 1d

An e-mail

1 a. Look at the web page. Who is it for?

b. Read the web page and underline the words that tell you which information to include in your e-mail.

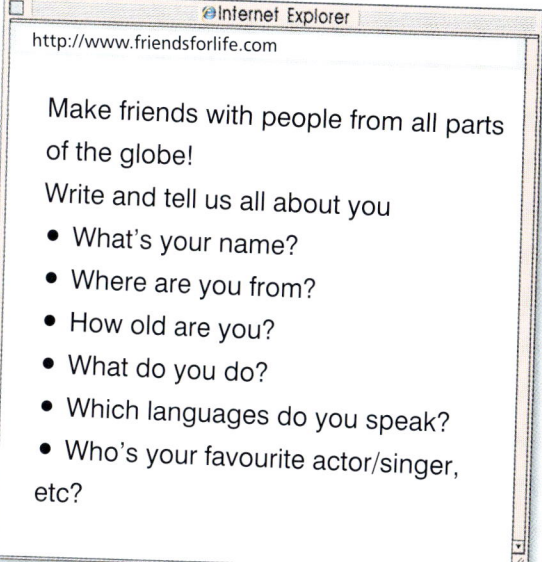

2 Read the following e-mail from Renate in Germany. Does she answer all the questions above?

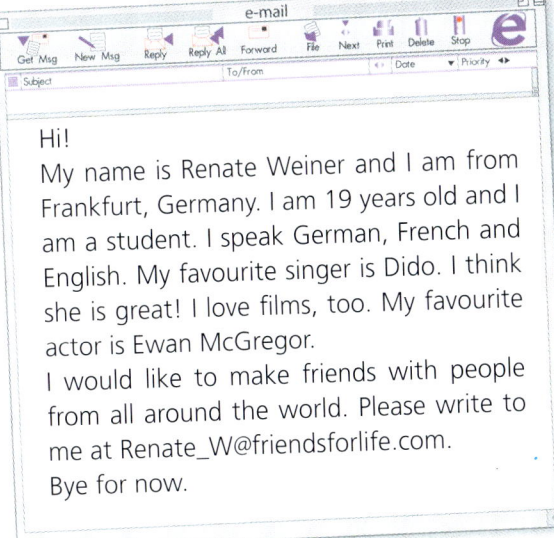

3 When we write a letter, e-mail, etc to a friend we use short forms.

My name is Renate.
My name's Renate.

Rewrite Renate's letter using short forms. Read it to the class.

4 Join the sentences, as in the example.

1 My name is Renate Weiner. I am from Frankfurt.
My name is Renate Weiner and I am from Frankfurt.

2 I love football. My favourite team is Real Madrid.
....

3 My favourite singer is Shakira. My favourite song is *Whenever, Wherever*.
....

4 My friend is from Mexico. She is 18 years old.
....

5 I like films. My favourite actor is Will Smith.
....

5 **Portfolio:** You want to make some friends from other countries. Write to friendsforlife.com. Use the e-mail in Ex. 2 as a model.

Read and choose.

- Where is Jennifer Lopez from?
  A Cuba
  B Puerto Rico
  C The USA

- In the word 'e-mail', 'e' means:
  A electronic
  B envelope
  C express

- Where is Waterloo?
  A France
  B England
  C Belgium

9

1 Grammar in Use

1 Read and complete the sentences.

Long form	Short form
1 What is your name?	What*'s* your name?
2 She is from England.	She .... from England.
3 John is not a student.	John .... a student.
4 We are sisters.	We .... sisters.
5 I am not twelve years old.	I .... twelve years old.
6 We are not at school today.	We .... at school today.

2 Fill in: *am*, *are*, *is*.

1 I *am* a girl.
2 My mother .... at work.
3 Felix and Trixie .... my cats.
4 Felix .... in the garden.
5 My pencils .... on the floor.
6 Susan and Betty .... good at sports.
7 I .... at home.
8 We .... friends.
9 It .... Monday.
10 .... they in Rome this week?

3 Fill in: *is/isn't*, *are/aren't*.

1 This *is* my best friend, Mary, from school.
2 My bag .... black. It is white.
3 We .... from Spain. We are English.
4 They .... very friendly. We like them.
5 She .... 18 years old. She is only 16!
6 This .... my dog. It .... a sheepdog.
7 They .... classmates. They go to different schools.
8 It .... raining. Take an umbrella.

4 Read and correct the sentences.

1 He ~~are~~ from Germany.   *is*
2 Is I late?   ....
3 They isn't here.   ....
4 Where is you from?   ....
5 She are 18 years old.   ....
6 It aren't yellow.   ....

5 Read and match.

1	How old are you?	a	P–E–N.
2	What's your name?	b	Bill.
3	Where are you from?	c	My friend, Sam.
4	How do you spell it?	d	Italy.
5	Who's this?	e	An Egyptian vase.
6	What's this?	f	17

1 *f*   3 ......   5 ......
2 ......   4 ......   6 ......

6 Complete the questions using the words below. Then, ask your partner and write his/her answers. You can use the words more than once.

• How • Why • Who • Where • What

1 A: *How* old are you?
  B: ....

2 A: .... is your favourite singer?
  B: ....

3 A: .... do you like doing in your free time?
  B: ....

4 A: .... is your last name?
  B: ....

5 A: .... is your best friend?
  B: ....

6 A: .... do you live?
  B: ....

10

7 Read and complete the dialogues. Then, write.

A

Alain: Brigitte, *who is* that over there? Do you know her?
Brigitte: That's my friend, Anita. She's from Britain.
Alain: ………………… old is she?
Brigitte: She's seventeen. Anita!
Anita: Hi, Brigitte. ………………… are you?
Brigitte: Fine, thanks. Anita, this is my friend, Alain. He ………………… from France, too.
Anita: Nice to meet you, Alain!

Alain and Brigitte are *French*, but Anita is ……………………………………… .

B

Eva: Hello, my name ……………… Eva. ……………………… your name?
Rosanna: Rosanna.
Eva: ……………… you from, Rosanna?
Rosanna: Madrid, Spain. And you?
Eva: ……………………… from Warsaw, Poland.

Eva ……………, but Rosanna ……………… .

8 Put the words in the correct order to make sentences.

1 Susan/from/is/where?
   Where is Susan from?
2 from/your parents/Italy/are?
   …………………………………………………………
3 is/your/this/brother?
   …………………………………………………………
4 he/an actor/is?
   …………………………………………………………
5 they/friends/are/your?
   …………………………………………………………
6 she/16 years old/is?
   …………………………………………………………

9 This is your pen-pal. Write a paragraph about her.

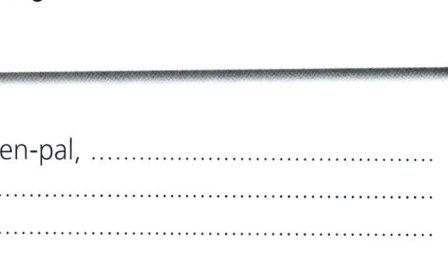

Name: *Adèle Bodart*
Age: *20*
Nationality: *French*
Favourite Food: *pizza*
Favourite Singer: *Britney Spears*

This is my pen-pal, ………………………………
She is ………………………………………………
……………………………………………………………
……………………………………………………………
……………………………………………………………
……………………………………………………………

1 Reader's Corner

1 a. What do you know about Penelope Cruz? Tell the class.

b. What questions would you like to ask her? Write them down. Then, read the interview quickly and see if there are any answers to your questions.

2 a. Read the interview and complete the questions.

An interview with Penelope Cruz

Interviewer: Penelope, 1) .... nickname?
Penelope: My nickname is Pe, it's short for Penelope.
Interviewer: So, 2) .... from?
Penelope: I'm from Madrid in Spain.
Interviewer: 3) .... is your birthday, Penelope?
Penelope: It's on the 28th of April.
Interviewer: 4) .... brothers and sisters have you got?
Penelope: A brother, Eduardo and a sister, Monica.
Interviewer: 5) .... are your favourite things?
Penelope: Dancing! I love classical and Spanish ballet. And I love animals, too!
Interviewer: 6) .... is your favourite food?
Penelope: Oh, Japanese food. I love it!
Interviewer: Thank you very much for giving this interview, Penelope.
Penelope: You're welcome.

b. Look at the pictures and talk about Penelope Cruz.

Project

3 Who is your favourite actor/singer, etc? Imagine you are interviewing them. Write down some questions you'd like to ask them. If you wish, you can find the answers to your questions on the Internet, in magazines, etc. Present your questions (and answers) to the class.

Progress Check

Vocabulary & Grammar

A Circle the correct item.

1 .... me an e-mail if you like.
   A Contact   B Drop   C Write

2 Jim and Linda .... the same age. He is sixteen and she is fourteen.
   A are   B aren't   C isn't

3 The Statue of Liberty is a famous .... in the USA.
   A capital city   B country   C landmark

4 Mei is from China. She is ....
   A Japanese   B Chinese   C Mexican

5 This is Ann. .... from Britain.
   A She's   B She aren't   C Is she

6 .... is your e-friend's name?
   A How   B What   C Whose

7 "What .... is he?" "Turkish."
   A nationality   B name   C country

8 Pièrre is .... France.
   A for   B to   C from

9 Nice to .... you, too!
   A write   B meet   C contact

10 How old .... ?
   A she is   B are she   C is she

11 Who's your .... singer?
   A nice   B favourite   C famous

12 My name's Timothy Stevens, but please .... me Tim.
   A call   B meet   C see

13 .... do you spell your name?
   A Whose   B Which   C How

14 .... are you?
   A Who   B What   C Which

15 We .... from the USA. We're American.
   A aren't   B is   C are

16 Warsaw is the .... of Poland.
   A country   B capital city   C landmark

17 He .... an actor. He's a singer.
   A is   B are   C isn't

18 .... exactly are you from?
   A What   B Where   C How

19 Sue and Pat .... at school.
   A am   B are   C is

20 This is a picture .... me and my best friend, Jill.
   A from   B for   C of

Communication

B Complete the exchanges.

a Pleased to meet you, Mrs Jones.
b Have a nice day!
c Hello, I'm Laura Taylor.
d Not bad. How are you?
e Nice to meet you, Jo!

1 A: ....
   B: Nice to meet you, Laura.

2 A: Hi, Steve. How are things?
   B: ....

3 A: Hi! My name's Joanna, but please call me Jo.
   B: ....

4 A: Mum, this is Olga. She's from Mexico. Olga, this is my mum.
   B: ....

5 A: Bye, Daddy. See you later!
   B: Bye-bye, Lin. ....

Total: _____
25x4   100 marks

13

2a Family ties

Vocabulary Practice

1 Look at Alice's family tree. Read the sentences and circle the correct word.

1. Jane is Lucy's younger **(sister)**/**aunt**.
2. Lucy hasn't got any **brothers**/**sisters**.
3. Eric is Simon's **uncle**/**grandfather** and Judith is his **grandmother**/**aunt**.
4. David's **brother's**/**father's** name is Tim and his **grandmother's**/**mother's** name is Pam.
5. Jane is John's **daughter**/**sister**.
6. Tim is Judith's **husband**/**son**.
7. Pam is Tim's **wife**/**daughter**.
8. Simon is Lucy's **brother**/**cousin**.

2 Fill in the correct word.

• call • age • fun • hit • member • meet

1. The new family series *Friends Forever* **hit** the TV screens this week!
2. Samantha is only six, but she's very clever for her ....
3. I'm Donna Gilbert and I'm a .... of the Gilbert family.
4. Frank, I want you to .... my mum and dad.
5. My dad's name is Matthew but most people .... him Matt.
6. My dogs, Jessie and Blackie, have a lot of .... together.

Reading

3 a. Who's the one? Read and choose.

She hasn't got long hair. She's got glasses. She's got curly hair. She hasn't got blue eyes. It's ...

b. Now, choose a picture and write your own sentences. Ask your friend to guess which picture.

They haven't got … . They've got … .

Families of the world 2b

Vocabulary Practice

1 Match the first column to the second one. Then, make sentences.

1	host	a	life
2	face	b	abroad
3	home	c	family
4	family	d	made
5	live	e	the world

2 a. Look at the following adjectives. Which adjectives refer to appearance (A)? Which refer to character (Ch)?

- kind   Ch
- overweight   A
- short   ......
- dark   ......
- pretty   ......
- clever   ......
- long   ......
- curly   ......
- tall   ......
- wavy   ......
- handsome   ......
- friendly   ......
- serious   ......
- funny   ......
- good-looking ......
- slim   ......
- fair   ......
- blue   ......

b. Describe three members of your family, as in the example.

My mother's name is Cathy. She's quite tall and pretty. She's got dark, curly hair and big, blue eyes. She's very kind and friendly.

3 Put the words into the correct box: *short, wavy, pretty, fair, blue, tall, handsome, straight, brown, curly, good-looking, overweight, slim*.

HEIGHT	EYES	HAIR	APPEARANCE
short			

Listening

4 🎧 Listen and choose.

- Which is Darek?

GAME

Your teacher pins the name of a famous person on your back. Find out who you are! Ask your classmates questions.

A: Am I a woman?
B: Yes, you are.
A: Have I got fair hair?
B: Yes, you have.
A: Am I slim?
B: Yes, you are.
A: Am I Claudia Schiffer?
B: Yes, you are!

15

2c Family fun!

Vocabulary Practice

1 a. Look, read and match.

1	h	play tennis	7		dive
2		ride a horse	8		ride a bike
3		swim	9		play baseball
4		surf the Internet	10		ski
5		cook	11		play chess
6		take photos	12		play football

b. What is the correct activity for each sentence? Read, choose and complete.

1 'Just click *search*. See? You can *surf the Internet*!'

2 'Don't worry, I can .... Say *cheese*, everyone!'

3 'I can ...., but the water is too cold today. Brr!'

4 'I can't ...., I'm afraid, but I can take you to a nice restaurant.'

5 'Checkmate! See? I can ....!'

6 'Goal! Wow! Patrick can .... really well.'

Everyday English

2 Read and choose. Then, take roles and act out.

1 A: Can you cook?
B: a That sounds good.
   b No, I'm hopeless!
   c Oh, really?

2 A: How can I help you, madam?
B: a I need some batteries for my clock.
   b Yes, please.
   c Why not?

3 A: Can you take our picture, please?
B: a It's very nice.
   b Where to?
   c Sure, no problem.

Speaking

3 Your whole family are at camp. Call your friend and tell him/her:

• the name of the camp
• what activities families can do there.

16

Writing 2d

Supreme Sports Centre

NOW OPEN

A **fabulous** sports centre the whole family can enjoy. We invite you to come and use our **wonderful** facilities:

- gym
- 2 **huge** swimming pools
- 2 indoor basketball courts
- aerobics studio
- 4 outdoor tennis courts
- the **trendy** Supreme Café

We're open seven days a week, providing hours of fun for all the family!

Next to the Sherman Hotel on East Street!

For more information, you can call us on 0161 232 9548

An ad

1 Read the ad and answer the questions.

1. What's the name of the sports centre? Where is it?
2. What facilities are there at the sports centre?
3. What can you do there?
4. What's their telephone number?

2 When we write an ad, we use adjectives to make our ad more interesting. Read the ad again and replace the words in bold with the adjectives below.

- fashionable • fantastic • big • excellent

3 Portfolio: You are the owner of a new sports centre. Write an ad for it to send to the local newspaper. Use the questions and the model in Ex. 1 to help you.

Trivia Time!

Read and choose.

1. Which famous pop star has got one green eye and one brown?
   A Elton John
   B Robbie Williams
   C David Bowie

2. What's the surname of the British Royal Family?
   A Windsor
   B Kent
   C Spencer

3. Who's David Beckham's wife?
   A Victoria
   B Beth
   C Diana

17

2 Grammar in Use

1 Look, read and complete.

Gwyneth Paltrow • Nicole Kidman • George Clooney • Antonio Banderas

1. Gwyneth Paltrow **1)** *is* from the U.S.A. She **2)** .... an actress. She **3)** .... fair hair and blue eyes.

2. Nicole Kidman **4)** .... from Australia. She **5)** .... an actress. She **6)** .... red hair and blue eyes.

3. George Clooney **7)** .... dark hair and brown eyes. He **8)** .... from the U.S.A. He **9)** .... an actor.

4. Antonio Banderas **10)** .... an actor. He **11)** .... dark hair and brown eyes. He **12)** .... from Spain.

2 Complete the sentences with *have/has got* or *haven't/hasn't got* and one of the following:

- a garage • eight legs • a key • five cats
- any money • a lot of friends

1. It's a big house, but it *hasn't got a garage*.
2. Jenny is very popular. She ....
3. He can't get into the house. He ....
4. Spiders ....
5. I can't go out tonight. I ....
6. Anna likes animals. She ....

3 Answer the questions about yourself.

1. Have you got any brothers or sisters?
   ....
2. What colour eyes have you got?
   ....
3. What colour hair has your dad got?
   ....
4. Have you got a pet? What is it?
   ....

4 Fill in: *have*, *haven't*, *has* or *hasn't*.

1. A: *Have* you got a brother?
   B: Yes, I ...., but I .... got a sister.
2. A: .... your dad got a moustache?
   B: No, he ....
3. A: .... she got a sister?
   B: Yes, she ....
4. I .... got three brothers and two sisters.
5. What colour eyes .... your mum and dad got?
6. Lisa and Mark .... got short, black hair.

5 Read and complete.

1. This is our daughter. *Her* name's Julie.
2. Is William at home? .... car isn't outside.
3. We live in the centre. .... house is in Bridge Street.
4. I haven't got .... own TV.
5. Is that .... new computer? You're very lucky!
6. Who are they? I don't know .... names.

18

6 Underline the correct word in bold.

1. Is this **you/<u>your</u>** book?
2. **His/He** favourite sport is football.
3. **I/My** party is on Saturday.
4. **They/Their** house is very big.
5. This is **our/we** classroom.
6. **She/Her** wedding is in July.
7. **He/His** sister is on holiday.
8. **They/Their** shoes are too small.

7 Look, ask and answer.

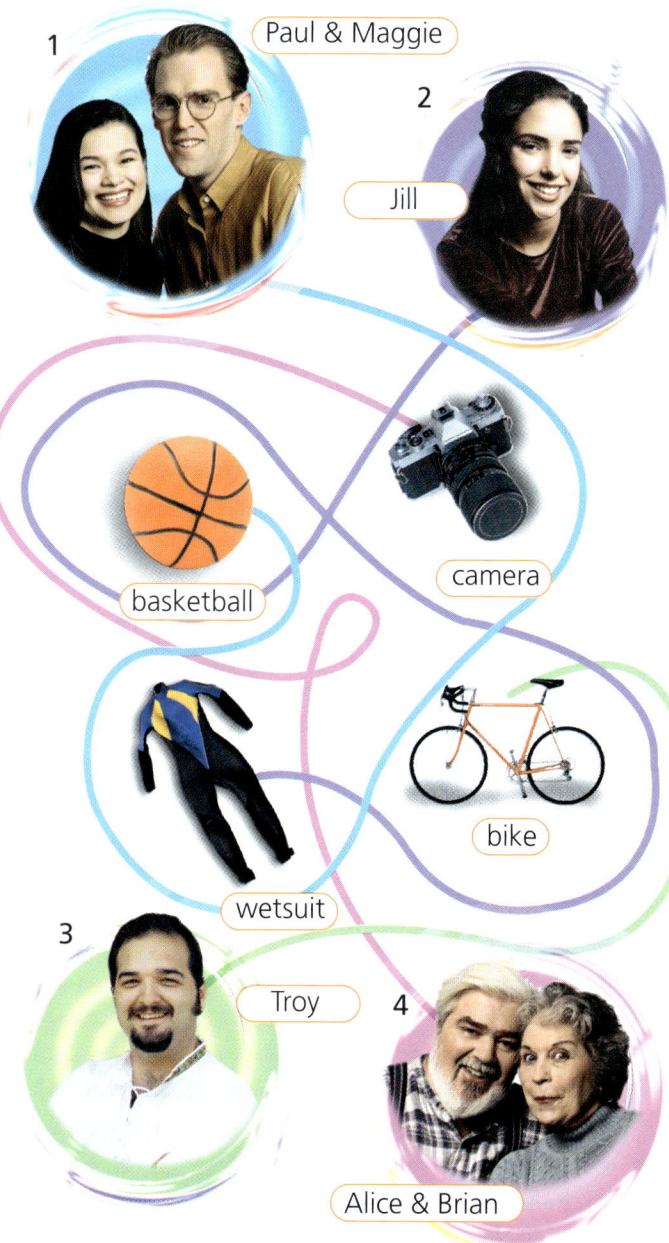

1. A: *Whose is the basketball?*
   B: *It's Paul and Maggie's.*

8 Which of these can/can't you do? Look and say.

1. I can/can't play tennis.

9 Complete the sentences. Use *can* or *can't* and one of the following verbs:

• come • eat • run • find • speak • play

1. I'm sorry, but I *can't come* to the cinema tonight.
2. Where's my pencil? I .... it anywhere.
3. The pizza is too hot. I .... it.
4. Let's go to the park. We .... football there.
5. Rose has got a lot of medals. She .... really fast!
6. Mrs Drake is in a meeting. She .... to you now.

19

2 Reader's Corner

My name is Leela Jaffray and I'm seventeen. I'm from Mumbai, India. There are five people in my family: my father, mother, two brothers and me. My parents are called Anand and Ramya. My father has got his own restaurant. My brothers, Ravi and Vijay, are teachers. And me? Well, I'm a student at Vijay's school – and I love cricket! In fact, we all love sports in my family! Our favourite food is vegetables, especially Baigan Bhartha! My family and I would love to welcome you into our home!

1 a. Look at the picture. Where do you think the family is from? How many people are there in the family?

b. Read and find the names of a: *country, sport, job, dish*.

2 Read again and say True or False.

1. Leela is seventeen years old.
2. There are five children in the Jaffray family.
3. Leela's father works in a restaurant.
4. Leela's favourite sport is football.
5. The Jaffray family loves fish.

3 You are staying with the Jaffray family. Tell a friend about them. Talk about: names, ages, jobs, favourite family activity, favourite food.

Progress Check

Vocabulary & Grammar

A Circle the correct item.

1 My aunt's husband is my ....
   A grandfather B uncle   C brother

2 Look at .... family.
   A Philip   B Philip is   C Philip's

3 She isn't fat; she's a little ....
   A overweight   B slim   C tall

4 Patty is only six, but she's very .... for her age.
   A lovely   B cute   C clever

5 Excuse me, is this .... pencil?
   A your   B you are   C you

6 We can .... a horse at the camp.
   A take   B ride   C play

7 We can start swimming. It's a good way to keep ....
   A fit   B fun   C happy

8 .... you play chess?
   A Can   B Have   C Are

9 Derek has got a .... and a moustache.
   A bird   B bag   C beard

10 Peter .... got a younger sister.
    A is   B have   C has

11 I like Helen's dark, ... hair.
    A slim   B wavy   C plump

12 Ben is tall and ....
    A handsome   B short   C pretty

13 Paul and Cathy are moving into .... own house.
    A they   B their   C they're

14 .... she got a big family?
    A Has   B Have   C Haven't

15 'Whose is this camera?' 'It's ....
    A Mary's   B Mary   C she

16 'Has she got a bike?' 'No, she ....
    A hasn't got   B hasn't   C has

17 We live in Spain. .... house is in Madrid.
    A Ours   B Our   C Your

18 Michael is Mr Dean's only ....
    A son   B sister   C daughter

19 Tim spends hours .... the Internet.
    A surfing   B playing   C skiing

20 My dad is great ....!
    A smile   B fun   C eyes

Communication

B Complete the exchanges.

a Can you help me with this exercise?
b Oh, hello. I need a disk for my computer.
c Good morning. How can I help you?
d Yes, of course. Where are the glasses?
e Sure, no problem.

1 A: Can you bring me a glass of water, please?
  B: ....

2 A: Good morning, how can I help you?
  B: ....

3 A: ....
  B: Sure, no problem.

4 A: ....
  B: Oh, hi. I need a film for my camera.

5 A: Can you answer the phone for me, please?
  B: ....

Total: _____
25x4   100 marks

21

3a Day by day

Vocabulary Practice

1 Look, read and complete the phrases.

1 .... homework
2 .... a lesson
3 .... breakfast
4 .... to school
5 .... the washing-up
6 .... a magazine
7 .... the shopping
8 .... the dog

2 a. Use the words in the list to fill in the table.

- a lesson • the washing-up • to school • breakfast • to the gym • jogging • homework
- to the cinema • the shopping

HAVE	DO	GO
a lesson	....	....
....	....	....
....	....	....
....	....	....
....	....	....

b. Which of these activities do you do a) in the morning? b) in the afternoon? c) in the evening?

I have breakfast in the morning.

22

School days 3b

Vocabulary Practice

1 Look at the pictures and find the school subjects.

1 M_t__ 2 __t 3 _u_i_ 4 E__l__h

5 __s___y 6 F___c_ 7 _c__n__ 8 G___r___y

2 Write the times.

 a  *five ten*/ten past five

 b two thirty/..............................

 c ..../a quarter to nine

 d five fifty/..............................

 e one fifteen/............................

 f  ..../twenty past four

Everyday English

3 Read and fill in. Then, act out.

- It's time for me to go • Yes, why
- What time is it

A: 1) ...., Sara?
B: I think it's about quarter past five.
A: Already?
B: 2) ....?
A: My dance class is at half past.
   3) ....!

Listening

4 🎧 Listen and tick (✓) the right answer.

1 What time is Sara's doctor's appointment?

A ☐ B ☐ C ☐

2 Where is Ben's Maths book?

  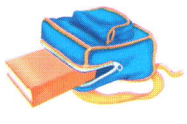

A ☐ B ☐ C ☐

3 Where does Michael work?

A ☐ B ☐ C ☐

4 What kind of holiday job does Nicole want?

A  ☐ B ☐ C ☐

3c Careers day

Vocabulary Practice

1 Fill in the puzzle. What's the extra job?

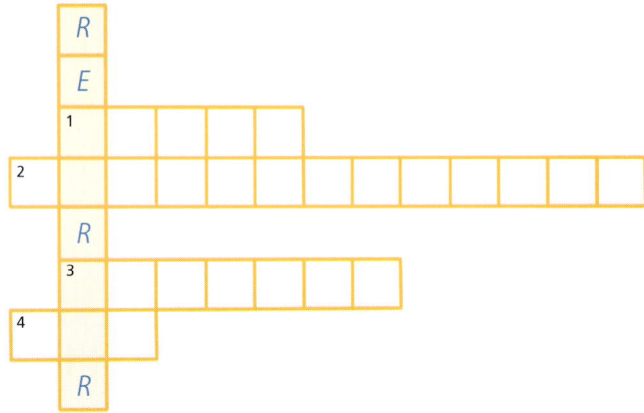

1 He flies planes.
2 This person protects the community.
3 This person works at a school.
4 You take your pets to this person.

What am I? In teams, take turns to mime a job.

Team A S1: (mimes writing on the board)
Team B S1: Are you a police officer?
Team A S1: No! (continues miming)
Team B S1: Are you a teacher?
Team A S1: Yes!

Speaking

2 Work in pairs. **Student A:** Look at the details of a chef's job and answer student B's questions.
Student B: Ask student A the questions about the chef's job.

Student A

I work at the Royston Hotel.
I work forty hours a week.
I decide what's on the menu every day. I prepare the main dishes.
I wear a white coat and hat.
I get £1,500 a month.

Student B

- Where/work?
- What/do?
- How many hours/work?
- What/wear?
- How much money/get?

Read and choose.

- Florence Nightingale was a famous
  A doctor.
  B nurse.
  C teacher.

- West Point in New York is a
  A military academy.
  B police academy.
  C naval academy.

- How long does a Rugby match last?
  A 90 minutes
  B 60 minutes
  C 80 minutes

24

Writing 3d

An article

1 Which of the following words are connected to a vet's job?

• surgery • cinema • medicine • operation • country • injection

2 a. Read the article and make notes about Michael's daily routine.

Michael Peterson is a vet. He works in a small town in Yorkshire, England.

Michael's day begins very early – at six o'clock. He gets up, has a quick breakfast, then gets into his car. In the mornings, he drives around the local farms to check on the animals – mostly cows, sheep and horses. At eleven o'clock, he goes to his surgery in the town. People bring their pets for Michael to look at. Most of the time, they only need an injection or some medicine, but sometimes they need an operation. Michael usually has lunch – a sandwich – standing up!

In the afternoons, Michael often goes to schools in the area to talk to the students about looking after their pets.

Michael's evenings are very quiet. He gets home quite late, cooks dinner and usually reads or watches TV. He goes to bed early, ready to face the next busy day.

In his free time, Michael likes going to the cinema or taking long walks in the country with his two dogs, Sheba and Nell.

Gets up: ....
In the morning: ....
At 11 o'clock: ....
Lunch: ....
In the afternoon: ....
In the evening: ....
In his free time: ....

b. Now, use your notes to talk about Michael's daily routine.

3 Which paragraph mentions the following? Read and write the number.

- What the person does in the afternoons: Paragraph ....
- What the person does in his free time: Paragraph ....
- The person's name, what their job is and where it is: Paragraph ....
- What the person does in the evenings: Paragraph ....
- What the person does in the mornings: Paragraph ....

4 Rewrite the sentences, as in the example.

1. He gets up. He has a quick breakfast. He gets into his car.
   He gets up, has a quick breakfast and then gets into his car.
2. She drives the children to school. She takes the dog for a walk. She goes to work.
   ....
3. He eats supper. He does the washing up. He reads the newspaper.
   ....
4. They arrive at the sports hall. They train for an hour. They have a friendly match.
   ....

5 **Portfolio:** Write about someone's daily routine. Use Exs 2 and 3 to help you.

25

3 Grammar in Use

1 Write, as in the example.

1 Sally and Ted *go to the cinema* on Sunday evenings.
   (go/the cinema)

2 Carol .... at Mortimer College.

   (study/Computer Science)

3 Bob and Patricia .... in the afternoon.
   (go/jogging)

4 Jeff .... on Saturday mornings.

   (play/baseball)

5 Richard .... in the afternoons.
   (meet/his friends)

6 Carla .... every Friday.

   (have/guitar lesson)

2 Use the prompts to write sentences, as in the example.

1 Mary/play/volleyball/on Saturdays.
  Mary plays volleyball on Saturdays.
2 They/visit/their parents/at weekends.
  ....
3 John/have/English lesson/every Monday.
  ....
4 On Sundays/she/have/breakfast/at 11:00.
  ....
5 We/go/shopping/every Friday.
  ....
6 He/study/for the exams/every day.
  ....
7 I/go dancing/on Thursdays.
  ....

3 Read and complete.

1 A: What time .... (your father/ start) work?
   B: He .... (start) work at 7:30 in the morning.

2 A: Where .... (your mum/work)?
   B: She .... (work) at Memorial Hospital.

3 A: .... (your parents/like) working with animals?
   B: Yes, they .... (both/love) animals.

4 A: .... (Simon/like) working long hours?
   B: No, it's quite tiring.

26

4 a. Look at the table and make sentences, as in the example.

	NEVER	SOMETIMES	OFTEN	USUALLY	ALWAYS
have coffee for breakfast					✓
do the washing-up				✓	
play video games	✓				
go to the gym		✓			
cook for friends			✓		
go to the cinema		✓			

Laura always has coffee for breakfast.

b. Talk about yourself. How often do you do these activities?

5 a. Fill in the gaps with the correct verb from the list in the *present simple*.

- have (x3) • get • leave • start
- wake up • drink • watch • do
- meet • finish • walk • go (x2)

Sylvia **1)** .... at 7:30 every day. She **2)** .... dressed, and then she **3)** .... breakfast. She **4)** .... the house at 8:30 and **5)** .... to school. School **6)** .... at 9 o'clock. She **7)** .... a lunchbreak from 12:15 until 1:15. School **8)** .... at 3 o'clock. Sylvia **9)** .... home at 3:20. She **10)** .... a glass of orange juice and then she **11)** .... her homework. After that, she **12)** .... her friends in the park. At about 8 o'clock she **13)** .... dinner. After dinner she **14)** .... TV. She usually **15)** .... to bed at 9:30.

b. Ask and answer *Yes/No* questions about Sylvia.

A: *Does Sylvia wake up at 7:00 every day?*
B: *No, she doesn't. She wakes up at 7:30.*

6 Correct the mistakes, as in the example.

1 She ~~like~~ cooking.   *likes*
2 He don't mind working
  at weekends.   ....
3 I are fit and strong.   ....
4 She likes work outdoors.   ....
5 He can rides a motorbike.   ....
6 Please you phone Jessie
  Parker on 5348291.   ....

7 Match the questions to the answers, as in the example.

1	*d*	Do you like your job?
2		What do you do on Sundays?
3		What time do you go to bed?
4		Where do you go on holiday?
5		When do you do your homework?
6		How do you travel to work?

a   At 10 o'clock.
b   In the evening.
c   By train.
d   Yes, I do.
e   To France, usually.
f   I always relax.

3   Reader's Corner

1 Do teenagers work part-time in your country? What kind of jobs do they do?

2 Read and fill in: *actors, children, parents, money, supermarkets.*

Working Teenagers

For teenagers in the USA, working part-time to earn some pocket money is very common.

In California, 1) .... of 12 and 13 can work but only as babysitters, paper boys/girls, gardeners, 2) .... or singers and only for three hours a day. Older children, 16 and 17 years old, can work longer hours and can work in 3) ...., fast food restaurants and as pizza delivery boys/girls.

Most teenagers say they work for a little extra pocket money and 4) .... usually agree that it is good experience for their children. They say that working part-time teaches young people about 5) .... and the real world.

3 Read again and answer.

  1 What kind of jobs can 12 and 13 year-olds do?
  2 Where can you work when you're 16 or 17 years-old?
  3 Why do most teenagers work?
  4 What does having a part-time job teach young people?

4 Use your answers from Ex. 3 to talk about part-time jobs for young people in California.

5 Interview some teenagers with part-time jobs. Ask them the following questions. Report your answers to the class.

  1 How old are you?
  2 Where do you work?
  3 How many hours do you work?
  4 How much money do you earn?
  5 What do you do with your money?

Progress Check

Vocabulary & Grammar

A Circle the correct item.

1. Helen .... Science at Chester College.
   A tries   B teaches   C likes

2. A .... is someone who takes care of sick animals.
   A pilot   B doctor   C vet

3. Diane .... to travel.
   A wants   B want   C is want

4. He likes .... video games.
   A play   B playing   C plays

5. It's ten o'clock .... the morning.
   A on   B at   C in

6. Tom doesn't .... working at weekends.
   A love   B mind   C know

7. Becky is good .... Maths.
   A at   B in   C to

8. She never .... to bed late at night.
   A go   B going   C goes

9. Which jobs are you interested ....?
   A on   B in   C at

10. I can .... a motorbike.
    A drive   B fly   C ride

11. Paul .... up at 10 o'clock on Saturdays.
    A gets   B goes   C be

12. .... you work in an office?
    A Does   B Do   C Doing

13. A reporter works .... a TV channel.
    A on   B in   C for

14. "Do you like working long hours?" "No, I ...."
    A like   B don't   C do

15. Phil plays sports because he wants to be .... and strong.
    A fit   B good   C sick

16. Kim has Maths .... Tuesdays.
    A on   B in   C at

17. A .... must be a good swimmer.
    A dog-walker   B babysitter   C lifeguard

18. Ron .... his teeth every morning and evening.
    A brush   B brushes   C is brush

19. Bill .... drive to work every day.
    A don't   B do   C doesn't

20. I must .... to the office for the meeting.
    A rise   B rush   C worry

Communication

B Complete the exchanges.

a What do you do in the afternoons?
b What's the time, Mandy?
c On Tuesdays.
d What do you want to be?
e It's seven forty.

1. A: What time is it?
   B: ....

2. A: When do you have History?
   B: ....

3. A: ....
   B: It's quarter past six.

4. A: ....
   B: I usually go to the park with friends.

5. A: ....
   B: A chef, because I like cooking very much.

Total: _____
25x4   100 marks

29

4a Fit for a Queen!

Vocabulary Practice

1 Match the rooms to the pictures.

    A living room   C bedroom
    B bathroom   D kitchen

2 a. Use the words below to complete the spidergrams.

- bath • pillow • armchairs • bedside table
- cupboards • sofa • sink • fridge • fireplace • bed
- coffee table • cooker • cushions • towels • curtains

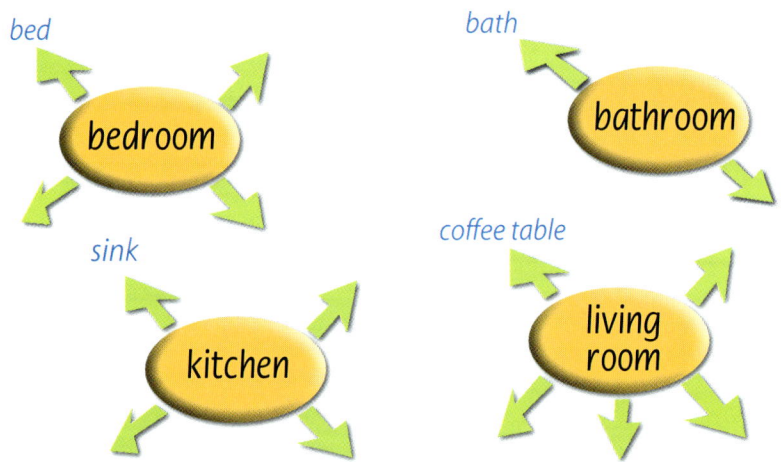

b. Use the words to describe your house.

Listening

3 🎧 Listen and complete.

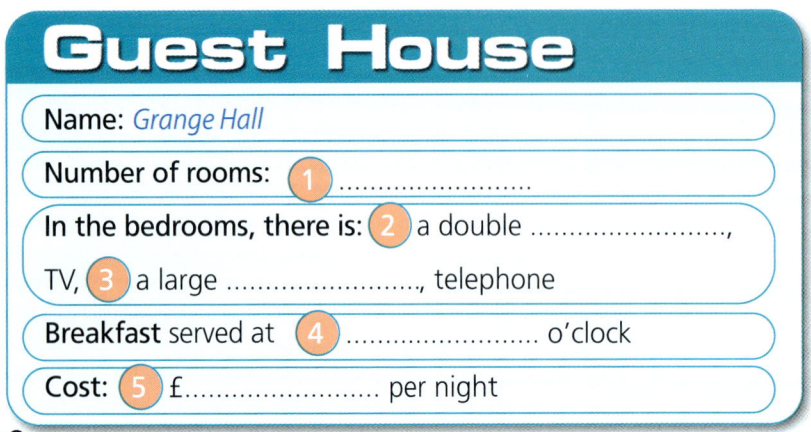

Guest House

- Name: *Grange Hall*
- Number of rooms: ①..................
- In the bedrooms, there is: ② a double ....,
- TV, ③ a large ...., telephone
- Breakfast served at ④ .... o'clock
- Cost: ⑤ £.................... per night

Reading

4 Read and write *A* or *B*.

A **Consort Road, SE15**
Large family home with three floors, four double bedrooms and two bathrooms. Garage, garden, spacious living room with fireplace and large, modern kitchen.
Tel.: 020 8981 9944 (9 to 5)

B **Alleyn Park, SE21**
Small studio apartment, close to city centre. Kitchen area with cooker and fridge. Small garden. Close to train station.

1. It is perfect for a family. ....
2. It is close to the shops. ....
3. It is near a train station. ....
4. It has got eight rooms. ....
5. It is a good place for a student. ....
6. It has got a place for a car. ....

Home exchange 4b

Vocabulary Practice

1 a. Match the types of houses with the correct pictures.

flat ☐   villa ☐   cottage ☐

b. Which one would you like to live in? Why?

2 Fill in the correct words, then write sentences.

• home • studio • tourist • fully-fitted • swimming • three-bedroom

1 *swimming* pool
2 .... kitchen
3 .... apartment
4 .... centre
5 .... exchange
6 .... flat

My house has got a large swimming pool.

3 a. Complete the crossword with the opposite of the adjectives.

1 small
2 cheap
3 unattractive
4 modern
5 busy

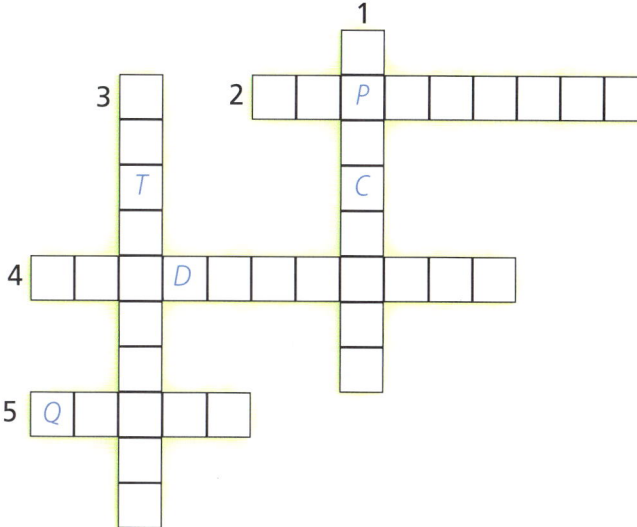

b. Complete the sentences using the adjectives from Ex. 3a.

1 This a _ _ _ _ _ _ _ _ flat is in a q _ _ _ _ street ten minutes from the city centre.
2 My house has got a s _ _ _ _ _ _ _ living room with a fireplace.
3 The villa is quite e _ _ _ _ _ _ _ _, but it is very large.
4 Kate has got a t _ _ _ _ _ _ _ _ _ cottage in Whitby.
5 My flat is quite big, but it is in a b _ _ _ area.

31

4c A new neighbourhood

Vocabulary Practice

1 Read and write the words.

1 People who like reading go here.   l _ _ _ _ _ _
2 This is a nice place to go to watch a film.   c _ _ _ _ _
3 You can buy fruit and vegetables here.   g _ _ _ _ _ _ _ _ _ _
4 People go here when they are sick.   h _ _ _ _ _ _ _
5 Children go here from Monday to Friday.   s _ _ _ _ _
6 People take their cars here.   g _ _ _ _ _
7 You can have a nice meal here.   r _ _ _ _ _ _ _ _ _
8 This is a good place to buy food for the family.   s _ _ _ _ _ _ _ _ _

2 Look at the map and answer.

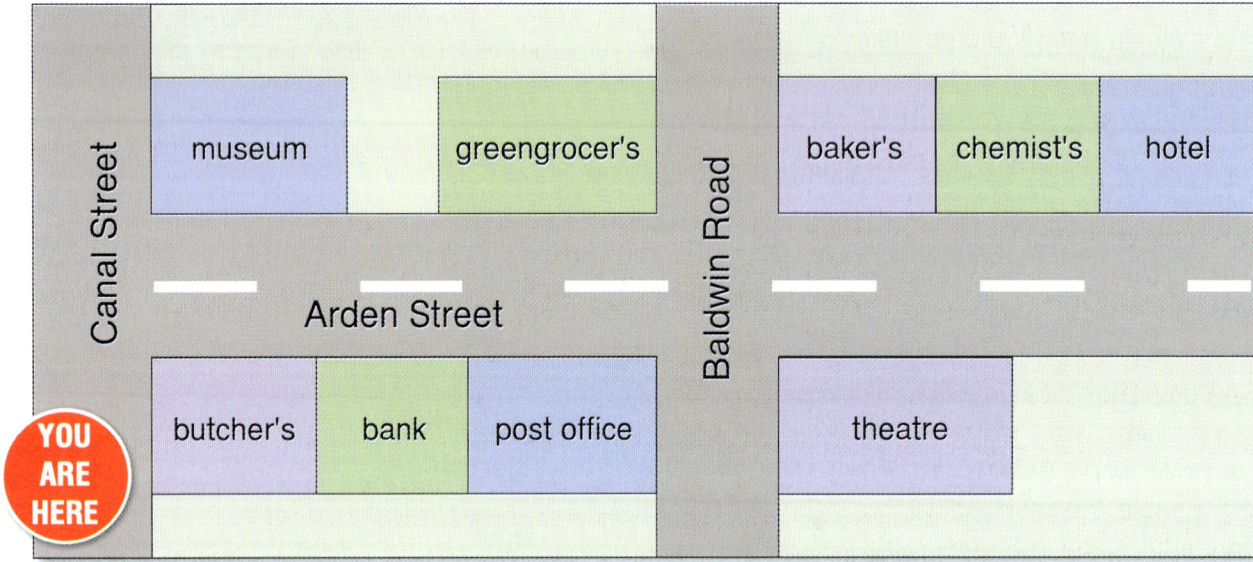

Where can you …
1 change money?
   At the bank.
2 buy stamps?
   ....
3 get a room for the night?
   ....
4 buy some vegetables?
   ....
5 order a birthday cake?
   ....
6 get something for a headache?
   ....
7 buy some sausages?
   ....
8 go to see a show?
   ....

Everyday English

3 Use the map to complete the dialogue.

A: Excuse me, where can I change money around here?
B: There's a bank in ....
A: How can I .... from here?
B: Walk along Canal Street and .... into Arden Street. The bank's on your right, next to ....
A: Thanks.
B: You're welcome.

4 **Portfolio:** Draw a map of your neighbourhood and present it to the class.

Writing 4d

An ad

1 Read the ad and answer the questions.

1. Where is the house?
2. How much is the rent?
3. What type of house is it?
4. What is it close to?
5. What rooms are there in the house?
6. What is there at the front and back of the house?

FOR RENT: £600/month
Address: 22, Hall Lane

This attractive two-bedroom house is in a quiet street near the city centre. It is in a very pleasant area and the rent is very reasonable. It has got two spacious bedrooms, two bathrooms with a toilet and shower, a modern kitchen with a cooker, fridge, washing machine and microwave oven, and a comfortable living room with a wonderful view of the park. There is also a large garage at the back of the house and a pretty garden at the front.

Call 01933 270586 for details.

2 Find the adjectives below in the text and fill in the nouns which are used with them.

1. quiet   ....
2. pleasant   ....
3. spacious   ....
4. modern   ....
5. comfortable   ....
6. wonderful   ....
7. large   ....
8. pretty   ....

3 The ad below is too long. It should only have up to eighty words in it. Read and decide which sentences to take out, then rewrite it.

FOR RENT: £350/MONTH
ADDRESS: 5, Linden Grove

This modern flat is in a pleasant street and is just five minutes away from the town centre. There are lots of shops in the town, where you can do your shopping. The flat is quite small, but the rent is very cheap for the area. It has got a pretty bedroom, a bathroom with a shower and toilet, a modern kitchen with a cooker, a dishwasher and a fridge and a very comfortable living room with a fireplace. Most people like to sit in their living rooms in the evening. The flat has also got a balcony at the front with a great view. You can see mountains and a lot of trees.

4 **Portfolio:** Write a *'For rent'* ad for your house. Complete the following:

FOR RENT (how much money a month): ....
ADDRESS: ....

- type of place: ....
- where: ....
- cost: ....
- size: ....
- inside the house/flat (rooms, furniture, etc): ....
- outside the house/flat: ....

Use the model in Ex. 1 to help you.

Trivia Time!

Read and choose.

- What can you see at 1600 Pennsylvania Avenue?
  A The Pentagon
  B The White House
  C The Statue of Liberty

- When you make your own things for your house, it's called ...
  A DHL.
  B DIY.
  C YHA.

- Who built the first hospitals?
  A The Egyptians
  B The Romans
  C The Babylonians

33

4 Grammar in Use

1 Read and choose the correct item.

1. Is my dictionary .... your bag?
   A at B between C in

2. He lives .... London.
   A under B on C in

3. There's a supermarket .... our flat.
   A opposite B under C between

4. I can't see the film. There's a tall man .... me!
   A next to B in front of C behind

5. Do you want to see my photos? Come and sit .... me.
   A behind B between C next to

6. The bank is .... the supermarket and the post office.
   A in B on C between

7. There's a cupboard .... the sink.
   A under B on C at

8. In Britain, people drive .... the left.
   A at B on C in

2 a. Complete the sentences with the correct prepositions of place.

1. Linda is *between* Sam and George.
2. The apple is .... the book
3. Terry is .... the swimming pool.

4. Laura is .... Jim.
5. Mr and Mrs Smith are .... their children.
6. Jill is .... Linda.

b. Look around you. Using prepositions of place describe the position of people and things in the room.

34

3 Write the plural.

1 spoon ....
2 plate ....
3 glass ....
4 shelf ....
5 carpet ....
6 house ....
7 wife ....
8 cottage ....
9 beach ....
10 knife ....
11 lake ....
12 room ....
13 fork ....
14 box ....

4 Rewrite the sentences.

1 There is a cup in the cupboard.
There are some cups in the cupboard.
2 Are there any forks on the table?
Is there a fork on the table?
3 There isn't a plate in the sink.
....
4 There are some books on the shelf.
....
5 There aren't any chairs in the room.
....
6 Is there a pen on the desk?
....
7 There are some boxes on the table.
....
8 Is there a boy in the room?
....

5 Look at the picture. What is there on the kitchen table? First say, then write.

1 *There is one plate on the table.*
2 ....
3 ....
4 ....
5 ....
6 ....

4 Reader's Corner

1 Where in your town/city can you do the following?

- buy souvenirs
- buy expensive gifts
- sit in a café
- shop on a Sunday

2 a. Read and complete the text. Use the sentences below.

A They can walk around and enjoy the sights and sounds of this busy street or shop at one of the 300 shops and department stores.

B There are also a number of wonderful cafés and restaurants to choose from.

Streetwise!

Oxford Street is a famous shopping area in the centre of London. People who visit Oxford Street never get bored. **1)** ....
Some of the shops in Oxford Street include Debenhams, Selfridges and Marks & Spencer. On Oxford Street, you can buy anything from expensive gifts to cheap souvenirs. Oxford Street is always full of people – even on Sundays when most of the shops are open. Need a break from all your shopping? **2)** ....
It's easy to see why Oxford Street is a big attraction for shoppers from all over the world!

b. Read the text again and complete the sentences. Then, talk about Oxford Street.

1 Oxford Street is in .... of London.
2 There are over .... shops and department stores.
3 You can buy lots of things there from expensive gifts to cheap ....
4 Oxford Street attracts .... from all over the world.

3 Work in pairs. Discuss a famous street in your country. Ask and answer questions about …

- the name of the street and where it is
- what kind of shops you can find there
- what else you can do there.

Progress Check

Vocabulary & Grammar

A Circle the correct item.

1 This villa costs a lot of money. It's very ....
   A expensive   B cheap   C quiet

2 There is a comfortable .... in the room.
   A mirror   B cooker   C sofa

3 The house has got a huge ....
   A garage   B curtain   C beach

4 There are five .... on the table.
   A knife   B knives   C knifes

5 There is a mirror .... the living room.
   A in   B on   C opposite

6 The cottage has got a(n) .... view!
   A picture   B amazing   C spacious

7 There .... two beds in the bedroom.
   A is   B has   C are

8 There are some lovely pictures .... the wall.
   A next to   B on   C behind

9 My flat is in a .... street, far away from the centre.
   A quiet   B busy   C modern

10 My parents live in a traditional .... by the sea.
   A road   B cottage   C block

11 The library is .... your right, next to the bank.
   A in   B under   C on

12 You can buy newspapers in a ....
   A newsagent's   B library   C baker's

13 I often stay at a .... when I'm on holiday.
   A guest house   B room   C tent

14 My flat has got a .... living room with a fireplace.
   A cheap   B spacious   C busy

15 There is a .... in the bathroom.
   A washbasin   B fridge   C cooker

16 The park is on the .... of Reed Road and River Street.
   A turning   B way   C corner

17 I keep my clothes in a big ....
   A wardrobe   B cabinet   C sink

18 .... some books on the table.
   A Are there   B There is   C There are

19 There are a lot of houses with beautiful gardens in Tony's ....
   A area   B flat   C building

20 There are three cars in the ....
   A garden   B staircase   C garage

Communication

B Complete the exchanges.

a Go along Morrison Avenue and turn right.
b It's in Wood Road, next to the baker's.
c Yes, there's one on Primrose Street.
d Do you know where the chemist's is?
e Can you tell me the way to the bank?

1 A: Is there a post office near here?
   B: ....

2 A: ....
   B: Sure. Walk along Rose Street, the chemist's is on your left.

3 A: Excuse me. How do I get to the library?
   B: ....

4 A: ....
   B: Walk along Pine Street. It's on the corner of Pine Street and Lewis Road.

5 A: Where's the supermarket, please?
   B: ....

Total: _____
25x4   100 marks

37

5a A matter of taste

Vocabulary Practice

1 Look and fill in the missing food items.

Vegetables

1 .... 2 .... 3 .... 4 .... 5 ....

Meals & Snacks

6 .... 7 .... 8 roast chicken and .... 9 ....

Desserts

10 chocolate cake 11 apple pie 12 .... salad 13 ....

2 What are your eating habits? Use the expressions to talk with your friend.

- like • love/be crazy about • hate/don't like

A: I like pasta and I'm crazy about chicken. I hate garlic, though. What about you?
B: Well, I like …

Listening

3 Listen and match the people to the star signs.

People	Star Signs
1 Dave	A Gemini
2 Graham	B Virgo
3 Penny	C Aries
4 Shelly	D Pisces
5 Maggie	E Cancer
	F Leo

What's on the list? 5b

Vocabulary Practice

1 Complete the sentences with words from the list.

- spoon • fork • plate • knife • frying pan
- saucepan • tin opener • cheese grater

1 We serve food on a *plate*.

2 We eat soup with a ....

3 We cut onions with a ....

4 We eat food with a ....

5 We fry eggs in a ....

6 We boil potatoes in a ....

7 We grate cheese with a ....

8 We open tins of food with a ....

2 Say the prices.

1 £3.45   4 £8.05
2 €5.50   5 €29
3 $9.80   6 $60.12

Three pounds forty five (pence).

3 Circle the odd word out.

1 a **carton** of orange juice/water/milk
2 a **slice** of bread/cake/butter
3 a **bottle** of cheese/lemonade/cola
4 a **packet** of flour/sugar/jam
5 a **cup** of tea/lemonade/coffee
6 a **jar** of jam/mayonnaise/crisps
7 a **bowl** of cake/soup/salad
8 a **tin** of tuna/pizza/beans

Everyday English

4 The following dialogue is in jumbled order. Put the sentences in the correct order, then act out the dialogue.

☐ And for the main course?
☐ Thank you, sir.
☐ I'd like the chicken curry and rice, please.
`1` Good evening, sir. Are you ready to order?
☐ A glass of cola, please.
☐ What would you like to drink?
☐ Yes, I'd like the vegetable soup to start with.

Trivia Time!

Read and choose.

- Where does Edam cheese come from?
  A France
  B Switzerland
  C The Netherlands

- Which explorers first brought potatoes to Europe?
  A Spanish
  B Portuguese
  C English

- What can you eat when you go to watch tennis at Wimbledon?
  A Fish and chips
  B Steak and salad
  C Strawberries and cream

39

5c What's cooking?

Vocabulary Practice

1 Look, read and match.

a b c d e

1. Peel a large onion, then chop it.
2. Fry the fish in a large frying pan.
3. Boil the water in a pot, then put the lobster in.
4. Grate some cheese over the pizza.
5. Grill the burgers and sausages on both sides.

2 Read and complete the sentences.

• crack • save • share • advice • mashed • water

1. Every time I peel onions, my eyes *water*.
2. First .... the egg into a bowl, then put it in the frying pan.
3. Do you prefer .... potatoes or chips?
4. Let's buy a ready-made salad. That way, we can .... time.
5. I always listen to his .... He knows everything about cooking.
6. My grandma gives me all her recipes. She likes to .... her secrets with me.

Speaking

3 Meg and Colin are having lunch in a restaurant. Meg is on a diet and Colin is a vegetarian. Read the menu and, in pairs, decide what they should eat.

A: I think Colin should have garlic bread as a starter.
B: I agree/I don't agree. I think he should have … .

Starters
Tomato soup
Tuna salad
Fried cheese
Garlic bread

Main Courses
– Steak served with baked potato or chips
– Cheese omelette
– Roast chicken, roast potatoes and vegetables
– Prawn curry and rice
– Vegetarian burger with green salad

Desserts
Chocolate cake
Fruit salad
Ice cream
Yogurt

Writing 5d

A restaurant review

1 Do you like Mexican food? Which of the following would you like to try?

- empanadas
- enchiladas
- tortillas
- burritos

2 Read the rubric and answer the questions.

> *You work for a local magazine. Write a review of a restaurant in your town.*

1. Where do you work?
2. What do you need to do?

3 Read the review and complete the table. Then, talk about the Santa Fe Mexican restaurant.

4 a. Read the text again and find adjectives which describe the following:

Food: *fresh*, ...
Service: ....
Atmosphere: ....

b. Rewrite the sentences below using adjectives from Ex. 4a to replace the word *'nice'*.

1. The food here is really **nice**.
2. Try some of this **nice** chicken curry.
3. All the waiters here are very **nice**.
4. This is my favourite restaurant. There's such a **nice** atmosphere.
5. Why don't you order the pasta. It's **nice**.

5 Portfolio: Write a review of a restaurant in your town. Use the table and the model in Ex. 3 to help you.

Santa Fe MEXICAN RESTAURANT

Santa Fe is a new Mexican restaurant in Chestnut Street. The owner's family run the restaurant so they take special care of all their customers.

The food is fresh and delicious and everything is homemade – even the tortillas are home-made! Try the chicken enchiladas with tomato sauce or the vegetarian empanadas with cheese and salsa. For those who don't like spicy food, there's a wonderful seafood pasta on the menu. For dessert, the cheesecake burritos are fantastic – or try the mango ice cream.

The service is friendly and fast and a meal for two people costs about £40. Santa Fe is open from 12 noon till 12 midnight. It is a good place to go for great food and a warm atmosphere, but it's very popular so you need to book a table.

Call 8926310
Have a wonderful meal!

Name/Type: *Santa Fe/Mexican restaurant*
Location: ....
Dishes: ....
Desserts: ....
Cost: ....
Service: ....
Opening hours: ....
Recommendation: ....

Santa Fe is a Mexican restaurant. It's in ...

5 Grammar in Use

1 Write C (for countable) or U (for uncountable).

1	milk	U	8	water	......
2	apple	......	9	coke	......
3	bread	......	10	potato	......
4	sandwich	......	11	sugar	......
5	coffee	......	12	egg	......
6	salad	......	13	butter	......
7	carrot	......	14	soup	......

2 a. Fill in *a*, *an* or *some*.

1. *an* apple
2. ..... cheese
3. ..... crisps
4. ..... tomato
5. ..... biscuits
6. ..... coffee
7. ..... egg
8. ..... chips
9. ..... orange juice
10. ..... milk
11. ..... bananas
12. ..... cherries

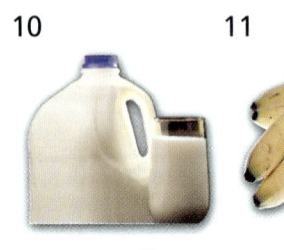

b. In pairs, using the nouns from Ex. 2a, ask and answer, as in the example.

A: *Would you like some orange juice?*
B: *Yes, please./No, thanks.*

3 Match column A to column B, as in the example.

	A		B
1 E	a glass of	A	eggs
2	a piece of	B	soup
3	a loaf of	C	spaghetti
4	a cup of	D	bread
5	a carton of	E	orange juice
6	a packet of	F	coffee
7	a jar of	G	cake
8	a bowl of	H	honey

4 Circle the correct item.

1. There isn't .... apple juice left.
   A some   (B) any   C an
2. Are there .... lemons?
   A any   B some   C a
3. Can I have .... milk, please?
   A any   B a   C some
4. Would you like .... chips?
   A some   B any   C a
5. Would you like .... sandwich?
   A some   B a   C an
6. There are .... peppers in the fridge.
   A any   B a   C some
7. I'd like .... cup of coffee.
   A a   B some   C any
8. There aren't .... tomatoes on the table.
   A some   B any   C an

5 Ask questions with *how much* or *how many*.

1. tomatoes/bag
   How many tomatoes are there in the bag?
2. sugar/packet
   ....
3. eggs/fridge
   ....
4. apples/basket
   ....
5. milk/fridge
   ....
6. bread/cupboard
   ....
7. orange juice/glass
   ....
8. mayonnaise/jar
   ....

6 Work with your partner. **Student A:** Cover the picture and ask your partner about: cheese, bananas, butter, coffee, apples, orange juice, jam, bread, eggs, cake, sugar, milk. **Student B:** Look at the picture and answer your partner's questions.

A: Is there much cheese left?
B: Yes, there's a lot of cheese.
A: Are there many bananas left?
B: No, there aren't many left.

7 Fill in *some*, *any*, *much*, *many* or *a lot*.

1. A: I'd like *some* eggs, please.
   B: How .... would you like?
   A: Five, please. Have you got .... milk?
   B: Yes. How .... do you need?
   A: One carton, please.
   B: That's €2.20.
   A: Here you are.
   B: Thank you very much.

2. A: Have you got .... oranges?
   B: Yes. How .... do you need?
   A: I need .... Can I have three kilos, please? Are there .... lemons?
   B: Yes, how .... would you like?
   A: Oh, not .... Just two.
   B: Here you are. Anything else?
   A: No, thank you.

8 Underline the correct pronoun.

1. Look at **he/him**.
2. **Her/She** has got a red dress.
3. Give the book to **me/I**.
4. Where are **them/they**?
5. Listen to **he/him**.
6. **I/Me** have got a car.
7. Do you know **they/them**?
8. **We/Us** are having breakfast.

9 Replace each word in bold with a subject or object pronoun, as in the example.

1. Joan likes bananas.
   She likes them.
2. Give **the cheese grater** to **Lin**.
3. **Jenny** is coming with **John and me**.
4. **This present** is for **you**.
5. **My brother and I** live near **you and Tim**.
6. **These shoes** belong to **Dave**.
7. **Alex** is talking to **those people**.
8. Is **this parcel** for **Kate**?

10 Fill in the correct subject or object pronoun.

1. "Do you know that man?" "Yes, I live next door to *him*."
2. I can't find my glasses. Where are .... ?
3. Come here, Betty! I need to talk to ....
4. We're going out. Do you want to come with ....?
5. I can't find my keys. I don't remember where I put ....
6. I like Mr Green. .... is very kind.
7. This is Ralph and I'm David. .... are brothers.
8. "Where's my pen? I can't find .... !"
9. "Is Nina with you?" "No, she isn't with .... She's in the living room."
10. I think we're lost. Where are .... ?

43

5 Reader's Corner

1 Can you name any foods from around the world? Write down as many as you can think of. You've got two minutes!

2 Label the pictures with the following words: *borscht*, *tortillas*, *kebab*, *pistachios*.

1 .... 2 .... 3 .... 4 ....

3 a. Do the quiz, but watch out – you might get hungry!

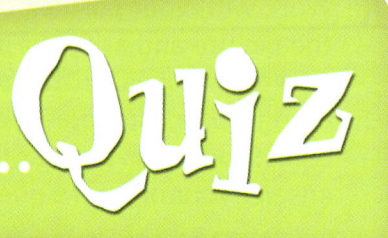

Quiz

1 Where can you get a five-course breakfast?
A France   B England   C Italy

2 Which country is famous for its delicious chocolates?
A Brazil   B Colombia   C Belgium

3 This is definitely a cheese country.
A Scotland   B India   C France

4 You can order borscht here.
A Russia   B Spain   C Portugal

5 Where are tortillas from?
A Sweden   B Mexico   C Poland

6 Sausages are a favourite here.
A France   B Japan   C Germany

7 This country is nuts about pistachios.
A Greece   B Egypt   C Argentina

8 Try a tasty kebab here.
A China   B Austria   C Turkey

b. In pairs, find information about food around the world and prepare your own quiz. Try it on another pair!

Progress Check

Vocabulary & Grammar

A Circle the correct item.

1. .... the onion, then chop it into small pieces.
   A Grate   B Peel   C Slice

2. I'd like a .... of tea, please.
   A cup   B jar   C slice

3. There aren't .... biscuits left.
   A some   B any   C an

4. Is there .... bread in the cupboard?
   A much   B many   C a lot

5. He has a .... of cornflakes for breakfast every morning.
   A packet   B bowl   C plate

6. Would you like .... cake with your coffee?
   A some   B a lot of   C a

7. We can have fish and chips for the main ....
   A dessert   B course   C starter

8. How .... milk is there?
   A many   B a lot of   C much

9. We eat soup with a ....
   A fork   B spoon   C knife

10. .... the pasta for 10 minutes.
    A Mash   B Fry   C Boil

11. We use a .... to peel potatoes.
    A spoon   B knife   C fork

12. .... the red pepper, onion and garlic.
    A Chop   B Grill   C Peel

13. There are .... of chocolates in the box.
    A many   B a lot   C much

14. Jim is very fond .... fruit.
    A for   B with   C of

15. I want something .... to eat. Is there any yogurt?
    A spicy   B hot   C light

16. As a .... I'd like some vegetable soup.
    A main course   B starter   C dessert

17. I don't like .... food. I prefer home-made food.
    A exotic   B fast   C expensive

18. Don't buy .... milk. We've got two cartons.
    A some   B any   C a

19. Can I have .... slice of cake?
    A an   B some   C a

20. I love .... food, especially curry.
    A perfect   B spicy   C junk

Communication

B Complete the exchanges.

a What would you like to drink?
b How much is it?
c No, thanks.
d I'd like the roast chicken with vegetables.
e OK, anything else?

1. A: Are you ready to order, sir?
   B: Yes, ...

2. A: ....
   B: A glass of Coke, please.

3. A: I'd like a cheeseburger and some chips, please.
   B: ....

4. A: ....
   B: That's £1.50.

5. A: Anything else?
   B: ....

Total: ——
25x4 100 marks

45

6a Weather blues

Reading

1 a. Where are they? Read and write the city.

CHICAGO
MOSCOW
CAIRO
LONDON

1. In .... today, it's raining as usual! I don't care though – I like it here!

2. I wish you were here in sunny .... It's boiling hot today, but we're sitting in a nice café!

3. .... is amazing! It's snowing today and it's very cold. We're on our way to the Kremlin.

4. No wonder they call .... the windy city! The wind is blowing really hard today!

Vocabulary Practice

2 Write the months.

WINTER
December
....
....

AUTUMN
....
October
....

SPRING
....
....
May

SUMMER
June
....
....

3 a. How does each person feel? Look, read and complete.

1 She's *happy*. (p p a h y)

2 She's .... (d s a)

3 He's .... (e p s t u)

4 She's .... (c e s d a r a)

5 He's .... (s e r d s t e s)

6 She's .... (e l d a x e r)

b. How do you feel when ... • it's hot and sunny? • it's raining? • it's windy? • it's snowing?

When it's hot and sunny, I feel happy and relaxed.

46

In action! 6b

Vocabulary Practice

1 Look and write.

1 He is *bungee jumping*.
2 She is ....
3 He is ....
4 They are ....
5 They are ....
6 They are ....

2 Look at the pictures and find the water sports.

Get your feet wet in Cancun!

Try some of the exciting water sports available!
- w _ _ _ _ –s _ _ _ _ _ _
- s _ _ _ _ _   d _ _ _ _ _ _
- w _ _ _ _ _ _ _ f _ _ _
- s _ _ _ _ _ _

Cancun, Mexico: the ideal place for some fun in the sun!

Listening

3 Listen to an advertisement about a popular winter destination and fill in the table.

Place: Whistler, British Columbia, Canada

What you can do there:

go 1 .... and snowboarding

2 .... a massage, buy souvenirs in a boutique

What you can do at night:

drink a 3 .... of hot chocolate, watch a film, have a delicious 4 ....

47

6c Just my style!

Vocabulary Practice

1 Look, read and choose.

1. A T-shirt
   B shirt
2. A skirt 
   B suit
3. A boots
   B shoes
4. A gloves 
   B tie
5. A shorts 
   B jeans
6. A trainers 
   B socks
7. A tracksuit 
   B coat
8. A swimsuit
   B raincoat
9. A glasses
   B scarf
10. A dress 
    B jacket

2 What do you think they should wear?

1. Jen's party is tonight and I want to look trendy.
   You should wear ....
   ....
2. I have a meeting with Mr Richards in his office.
   ....
   ....
3. It's snowing and I want to go out.
   ....
   ....
4. I want to go jogging.
   ....
   ....
5. Oh no, it's raining!
   ....
   ....

Everyday English

3 a. Use the questions below to fill in the gaps.

• Could I try them on • What do you think • How much are they • Can I help you

A: Hello. **1)** *Can I help you*?
B: Well, I'm looking for a pair of jeans but not too expensive.
A: These are nice and they're on sale – 40% off.
B: Great! **2)** ....?
A: Sure, the fitting room is over there.
B: Thanks.
A: **3)** ....?
B: Mmm, I'm not so sure. I think they're too big.
A: Let me see if I have a smaller size.
B: These are a better fit. **4)** ....?
A: £50. How would you like to pay?
B: Do you take credit cards?
A: Of course.

b. In pairs, act out similar dialogues, using the prompts below.

• dress • shirt • tracksuit • jacket • shoes • T-shirt

48

Writing 6d

A postcard

1 Look at the picture. Where do you think the people are? What's the weather like? Which words come to mind when you look at the picture?

Dear Robert,

Here I am in the Swiss Alps! I'm having a fantastic time.

I'm waiting to have my first skiing lesson and it's snowing quite heavily today. Alan is still eating breakfast – he loves the food here!

There are a lot of people on the slopes today. There's a little girl outside putting on her skis. She looks about three years old! The ski instructor is waving at me – I think it's time for my lesson now … wish me luck!

Bye for now. See you soon!
Lucy

Robert Mellors
48, Lower Baggot St
Dublin 2
Ireland

2 Read the postcard and answer the questions.

1. Who is Lucy sending the postcard to?
2. Where is she?
3. What is she doing?
4. What's the weather like?
5. Who is she on holiday with?
6. What's he doing?
7. What can she see outside?
8. Who is waving at her?

3 In which paragraph…

1. does Lucy give her closing remarks? Para: ……..
2. does Lucy say where she is and what she's doing? Para: ……..
3. does Lucy give more information about people, activities, etc? Para: ……..

4 a. Read the following sentences and write *O* for *opening remarks* or *C* for *closing remarks*.

1. How are you? We're having a great time here in Switzerland! ……..
2. Well, that's all for now. Time to go! ……..
3. We'll see you when we get back. Take care! ……..
4. I'm writing from the Swiss Alps! Wish you were here – it's great! ……..

b. Replace the opening and closing remarks in bold from Lucy's postcard with one from Ex. 4a.

5 Portfolio: Write a postcard to a friend from holiday. Use the model in Ex. 2 and the paragraph plan in Ex. 3 to help you.

Trivia Time!

Read and choose.

- Which scale is used to measure wind?
  A Mercali
  B Richter
  C Beaufort

- Who invented denim jeans?
  A Lee Cooper
  B Levi Strauss
  C Coco Chanel

- When does the football season officially end in England?
  A March
  B August
  C May

49

6 Grammar in Use

1 Read the postcard and put the verbs in brackets into the *present continuous*.

Dear Jerry,
   Majorca is great! I can't believe I'm here. Kathy, the kids and I 1) *are having* **(have)** the time of our lives. The weather is perfect – hot and sunny.
   We 2) .... **(stay)** at a fantastic hotel next to the sea. I 3) .... **(relax)** by the pool and enjoying a delicious fruit juice. Kathy 4) .... **(water-ski)**. I can actually see her from here, she 5) .... **(wave)** at me. Becky 6) .... **(take)** scuba diving lessons and Mark 7) .... **(windsurf)**. It's a dream come true!
   See you when we get back.
   Jack

2 Correct the false sentences, as in the example.

1 Becky is windsurfing.
   No, she isn't. She is taking scuba diving lessons.
2 Jack is writing from Ibiza.
   ....
3 Mark is relaxing by the pool.
   ....
4 Kathy is drinking fruit juice.
   ....

3 Use the verbs in the list to ask and answer questions, as in the example.

• ride a bike • water-ski • snowboard • run
• play basketball

1 A: What is he doing?
   B: He's snowboarding.

50

4 Ask and answer, as in the example.

1. Jane/watch/TV/now? – Yes
   A: *Is Jane watching TV now?*
   B: *Yes, she is.*

2. Tim/have/a bath/right now? – No/have/lunch
   A: *Is Tim having a bath right now?*
   B: *No, he isn't. He's having lunch.*

3. you/do/your homework/at the moment? – Yes
   A: ....
   B: ....

4. Dad/read/a newspaper/now? – No/water/the flowers
   A: ....
   B: ....

5. Helen/wash/her hair/at the moment? – No/tidy/her room
   A: ....
   B: ....

6. Kim and Sue/cook/now? – Yes
   A: ....
   B: ....

5 Complete the table.

Adjective	Comparative
good	better
comfortable	....
bad	....
....	more expensive
cheap	....
....	more fashionable
big	....
....	nicer

6 Read and complete.

1. Karen's boots are .... (expensive) than Cindy's.
2. That green tie doesn't go with your suit. It's .... (bad) than the grey one.
3. You can't wear my shoes. Your feet are .... (big) than mine.
4. My blue trousers are .... (long) than my red ones.
5. Long coats are .... (good) than short ones in the winter.

6. Your dress is .... (short) than mine.

7 Write sentences, as in the example.

1. Cathy's boots are very cheap.
   Yes, they're cheaper than mine.
2. Simon's jacket is very expensive.
   ....
3. Joanna's coat is very warm.
   ....
4. Luke's sunglasses are very modern.
   ....
5. Faye's blouse is really nice.
   ....
6. Mandy's shoes are very comfortable.
   ....

8 Use the appropriate form of the adjectives in the list to fill in the gaps.

- expensive • young • modern • fast

1. A motorbike is .... a bike.

2. John's jacket is .... Sam's.

3. Jill is .... Betty.

4. Tom's car is .... Bob's.

51

6 Reader's Corner

1. What kind of clothes do you wear in hot weather? Tell the class.

2. a. Look at the words in bold. They are all parts of the body. Point to them and say the words aloud.

   b. Read the article and label the pictures: *sari, salwar, kameez, sherwani, kurta-pyjama*.

Clothes in India

Indian clothes are popular for their bright colours and variety. Traditional Indian clothes are cool, comfortable and suitable for the hot climate.

Most women in India wear traditional clothes such as a sari or salwar kameez. A sari is a piece of cloth, usually silk or cotton, which is five to seven yards long. The women wrap the sari around their body, with the end of it left hanging or put over the **head**. Another popular item of clothing is the salwar kameez. The salwar is a pair of loose-fitting trousers with a tight fit around the **ankles**. The kameez is like a long shirt that comes down to the **hips** or **knees**.

Many men in India now wear western clothes such as shirts and trousers, but you can still see a lot of men in traditional clothes. Popular items for men are the sherwani and the kurta-pyjama. The sherwani is like a long, knee-length coat with buttons down the front. The kurta-pyjama is a knee-length shirt with no collar (kurta) and a pair of loose trousers that tie with a string at the **waist** (pyjama).

3. Read the article again and choose the correct answer.

   1. Indian clothes are suitable for the hot climate because they're ...
      A bright and colourful.
      B cool and comfortable.

   2. A sari is ...
      A a piece of silk or cotton cloth.
      B a type of coat.

   3. Salwar kameez is ...
      A a long skirt.
      B a shirt with trousers.

   4. Many men in India wear ...
      A long clothes.
      B western clothes.

   5. Popular items of clothing for men are ...
      A the sherwani and kurta-pyjama.
      B the sari and salwar kameez.

4. You own a fashionable Indian clothes shop. Tell a customer about the items of clothing you sell. Talk about:
   - the type of clothes you have for women and what they look like,
   - the type of clothes you have for men and what they look like.

5. **Portfolio:** Find pictures of traditional clothes in your country. Write a short paragraph about them. Say who wears them and when they wear them.

Progress Check

Vocabulary & Grammar

A Circle the correct item.

1 It's .... hot today.
   A boiling   B sunny   C freezing

2 What do you .... of this dress?
   A like   B think   C say

3 'Can I help you?' 'Yes, ...'
   A I'd like   B please   C I like it

4 'I'm .... some things for my trip.'
   A putting   B packing   C looking

5 What's the weather .... today?
   A cold   B doing   C like

6 This coat is half .... It's very cheap.
   A price   B money   C cost

7 The blue dress is smaller .... the red one.
   A of   B from   C than

8 Can I try this skirt .... ?
   A on   B at   C in

9 It's snowing and it's freezing ....
   A hot   B cold   C chilly

10 March, April and May are .... months.
   A winter   B summer   C spring

11 Dave is .... in the mountains.
   A camp   B camping   C camps

12 Do you .... Visa?
   A accept   B have   C like

13 Have you got this dress in .... ?
   A medium   B big   C middle

14 Ann is wearing a .... round her neck.
   A skirt   B jacket   C scarf

15 The weather is hot and .... today.
   A chilly   B windy   C sunny

16 Bob likes wearing trainers because they are ....
   A horrible   B comfortable   C handy

17 Mr Parker wears a .... because he works in an office.
   A tracksuit   B T-shirt   C suit

18 Boots are .... than trainers in the snow.
   A better   B worse   C good

19 They .... TV now.
   A watch   B is watching   C are watching

20 December, January and February are .... months.
   A autumn   B winter   C spring

Communication

B Complete the exchanges.

a Can I help you?
b It's really trendy. Do you have one in dark brown?
c Yes, of course.
d How much are these shoes?
e Have you got this blouse in medium?

1 A: ....
   B: They're £40.

2 A: ....
   B: Certainly, madam.

3 A: ....
   B: Yes, I'm looking for a long dress.

4 A: Do you accept credit cards?
   B: ....

5 A: This jacket is half price.
   B: ....

Total: ──── 25x4 100 marks

53

7a Charmed lives

Vocabulary Practice

1 Write the ordinal numbers.

1	one	–	*first*	7	twenty-one	–	....
2	two	–	....	8	thirty	–	....
3	three	–	....	9	thirty-three	–	....
4	four	–	....	10	sixty-nine	–	....
5	eight	–	....	11	ninety	–	....
6	twelve	–	....	12	a hundred	–	....

2 Write the years.

1 1657 ....
2 1730 ....
3 1869 ....
4 1993 ....
5 2005 ....

3 a. In pairs, ask and answer, as in the example.

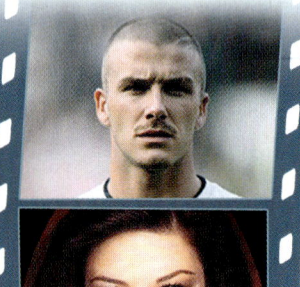

David Beckham
2nd May, 1975

Catherine Zeta-Jones
25th September, 1969

Tom Hanks
9th July, 1956

Bill Clinton
19th August, 1946

Madonna
16th August, 1958

Trivia Time!

Read and choose.

- Who played Conan the Barbarian?
  A Arnold Schwarzenegger
  B Sylvester Stallone
  C Roger Moore

- Which famous doctor travelled through time in a time machine?
  A Dr Doolittle
  B Dr Jekyll
  C Dr Who

- Why do American footballers paint black marks across their cheeks?
  A To protect them from the sun.
  B To look good.
  C To look scary.

A: When was David Beckham born?
B: He was born on the second of May, 1975.

b. When were you born?

I was born on …

The way it was! 7b

Vocabulary Practice

1 Look at the picture and write the words.

• buffalo • campfire • deer • drum • bow • arrows • tepee

2 Complete the spidergrams with the words below. Then, use any five to make sentences.

• seals • igloo • tepee • tent • whales • spears • polar bears • bows • caribou • arrows
• deer • buffalo

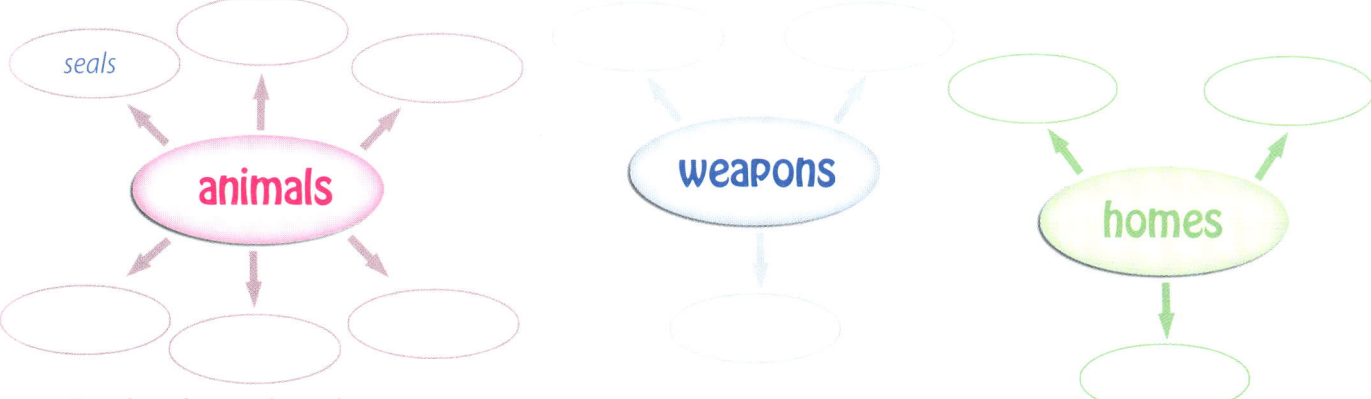

animals — *seals*

weapons

homes

3 Read and complete the sentences.

• grown-ups • greeted • hunt • memories • gathered • caring • dreamed • rhythm

1 Ted .... that he won the lottery.
2 He liked to .... rabbits.
3 The .... stayed inside while the children played in the garden.
4 Our host .... us at the door.
5 John had happy .... of his father.
6 They danced to the .... of the drums.
7 Peter is a loving, ... husband.
8 We .... firewood for the campfire.

55

7c It's all in the past!

1 Which picture shows: a wildlife programme? a sports programme? a comedy? a western?

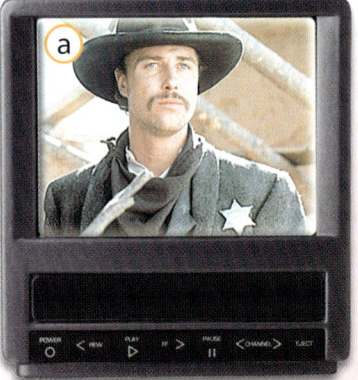

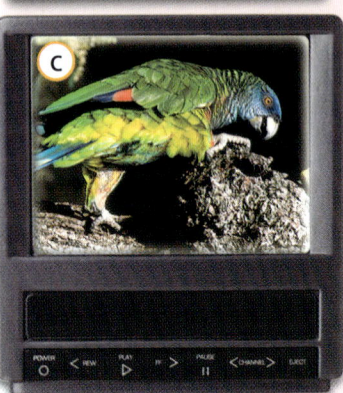

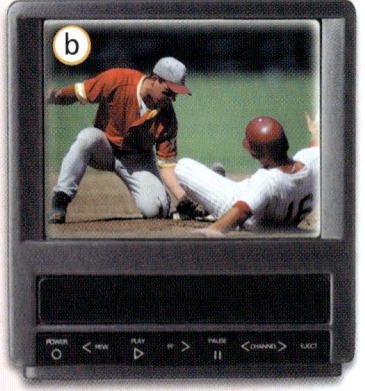

a
b
c
d

Listening

2 🎧 What did they watch on TV last night? Listen and match the people to the programmes.

People
1. Carl
2. Rosie
3. Ted
4. Cindy
5. Elaine

Programmes
A a play
B a soap opera
C a wildlife programme
D a sports programme
E a comedy
F a western

Speaking

3 Work in pairs. **Student A:** You are a member of Tom Hanks' fan club. Answer student B's questions. **Student B:** Ask student A your questions.

Student A

Join us and find out everything about this famous film star!

Tom Hanks' FAN CLUB

- Born in Concord, California – 9th July, 1956
- First big part in 'Splash'
- 1988: married Rita Wilson
- Two Oscars: Philadelphia – Forrest Gump
- 1996: directed first film, 'That Thing You Do!'
- 1997: travelled to Europe to film 'Saving Private Ryan'

27, Mill Street, London
Tel: 9426758

Student B

- when/Tom Hanks/born?
- what/first big part?
- who/marry?
- when/direct first film? title?
- where/travel/in 1997? Why?
- fan club address? telephone?

Everyday English

4 Choose the phrases from the list to complete the dialogue.

- Did you have a good weekend
- Really hectic
- No, I didn't
- It was a complete disaster
- How was your

Bob: Hi, Lin! 1) .... weekend?
Lin: 2) ....!
Shopping, cleaning, cooking. We had a dinner party on Saturday evening. What about you, Bob? 3) ....
....?
Bob: 4) .... !
Lin: Why? What happened to you?
Bob: Don't ask! I fell, hurt my ankle and missed my tennis match!
Lin: Oh, no! I'm really sorry!

Writing 7d

An article about a town 'then' and 'now'

1 What were seaside towns like in your country years ago? Tell the class.

2 Read the article and match the phrases to the pictures.

… *stand at the harbour and watch the cross channel steamers*
… *music hall stars used to entertain in the pavilion at the end of the pier*
… *take in the sea air and walk along the sea front*

A hundred years ago, Folkestone in the south of England was a popular resort for rich people.

People went to Folkestone to take in the sea air and walk along the sea front. The Victorian Pier was the most popular place to go, and famous music hall stars used to entertain in the pavilion at the end of the pier. In the old days, people used to stand at the harbour and watch the cross channel steamers coming and going.

Nowadays, most people spend their holidays abroad so there aren't as many holidaymakers in Folkestone as there used to be. There are playgrounds and amusement parks now – the pier and the pavilion aren't there any more. These days, people only go to Folkestone for the Channel Tunnel so they can travel over to France for the day.

Folkestone was such a beautiful place to go a hundred years ago. It's still a pretty fishing town, but many of its attractions are, sadly, lost forever.

3 Read the article and match the following phrases:

1 Channel   a air
2 amusement   b place
3 fishing   c Tunnel
4 beautiful   d parks
5 sea   e town

4 Read the article again and make notes.

Paragraph 1 – name of place: ....

Paragraph 2 – what life was like then: ....

Paragraph 3 – what life is like now: ....

Paragraph 4 – impressions: ....

5 **Portfolio:** Write an article for a magazine about a town now and then. Use the model in Ex. 2 and the plan in Ex. 4 to help you.

7 Grammar in Use

1 In pairs, ask and answer questions, as in the example.

1. you/cinema
2. Rick/park
3. Cathy and Brad/restaurant
4. The Parkers/theatre
5. Karen/home
6. Pam and Nick/work
7. Peter/gym
8. Garry and Ann/supermarket

1 A: *Where were you at 7 o'clock yesterday?*
   B: *I was at the cinema.*

2 Fill in *was*, *were*, *wasn't* or *weren't*.

1. A: How *was* the party last night? .... it fun?
   B: Yes, it .... great.
2. A: .... you with Jim last night?
   B: No, I .... I .... at home.
3. A: Where .... the children yesterday?
   B: They .... at the cinema.
4. A: .... you and Bill at home yesterday evening?
   B: No, we .... We .... out.
5. A: Where .... Tom and Jean last week?
   B: They .... in Spain.
6. A: .... you with Jill and Tony yesterday?
   B: No, I .... Pat .... with them. I .... at work.

3 Use *in*, *on* or *at* for each of the words or phrases.

- *in* May • ..... Mother's Day • ..... Wednesday
- ..... 5 o'clock • ..... summer • ..... 28th June
- ..... 2002 • ..... the morning
- ..... September • ..... New Year's Day
- ..... the moment • ..... the weekend
- ..... 14th March • ..... 1985 • ..... 12 o'clock
- ..... Valentine's Day • ..... Monday
- ..... the evening • ..... winter • 1996
- ..... spring • ..... 7th November

4 Fill in *at*, *in* or *on*.

1. My sister was born .... 1995.
2. The accident happened .... 10 o'clock yesterday morning.
3. Tom phoned his mother .... Mother's Day.
4. We visited our grandparents .... the weekend.
5. Kim and I played tennis .... Friday.
6. My parents moved house .... May.
7. Neil Armstrong landed on the moon .... 20th July, 1969.
8. Linda watched a video ..... 5:15 yesterday afternoon.

5 Write the *past simple* of the verbs.

1. walk – *walked*
2. watch – ....
3. dance – ....
4. cry – ....
5. turn – ....
6. play – ....
7. close – ....
8. stop – ....
9. study – ....
10. travel – ....
11. move – ....
12. tidy – ....

6 Make sentences using the prompts below, as in the example.

1. Janet's house is tidy.
   (tidy it/three hours ago)
   She tidied it three hours ago.
2. Julie's room is clean.
   (clean it/yesterday)
   ....
3. Bob and Liz don't live here anymore.
   (move to new house/last week)
   ....
4. John loves his new CD.
   (listen it/last night)
   ....
5. Kim is back from her holiday.
   (travel Spain/last week)
   ....
6. David isn't listening to music.
   (turn off radio/an hour ago)
   ....
7. Olivia is eating the cake.
   (bake it/an hour ago)
   ....
8. Rob doesn't go to the gym anymore.
   (stop going/two months ago)
   ....

58

7 Look at the pictures and answer the questions.

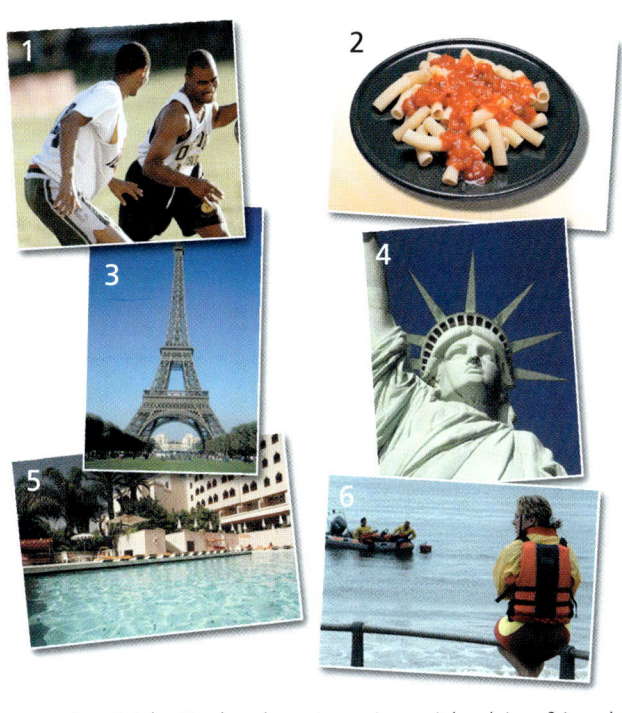

1. Did Carl play tennis with his friends yesterday afternoon?
   No, he didn't. He played basketball.
2. Did Mandy cook chicken yesterday?
   ....
3. Did Dave visit Rome last year?
   ....
4. Did Ron live in London as a child?
   ....
5. Did Barbara stay at a campsite last summer?
   ....
6. Did Debbie work as a waitress last year?
   ....

8 Put the verbs into the *past simple*, then match the questions to the answers.

1. ☐ Which programme .... (you/watch) at 8 pm on Saturday?
2. ☐ When .... (the Johnsons/travel) to Australia?
3. ☐ What .... (she/cook) for lunch?
4. ☐ Who .... (Michelle Pfeiffer/star) with in the film "What Lies Beneath"?
5. ☐ Where .... (they/stay) last summer?
6. ☐ Which sport .... (you/play) last week?

a In a hotel.
b Spaghetti.
c Love Boat.
d Badminton.
e Two years ago.
f Harrison Ford.

9 Jim Lloyd won a lot of money on the lottery last year. Look at the prompts and say what Jim used to do and what he does now.

THEN	NOW
• live in a small house • have a cheap car • buy cheap clothes • eat at home • go to work by train • spend his holidays at a campsite	• live in a large house • have an expensive car • buy expensive clothes • eat in restaurants • go to work by car • stay at luxurious hotels

Jim used to live in a small house, but now he lives in a large house.

10 Rewrite each person's comment using *used to* or *didn't use to*, as in the example.

Nora: I don't take the train to work any more.
   1) *I used to take the train to work.*

Bob: I go to the gym every day.
   2) ....

Kate: I like cooking now.
   3) ....

Sam: I don't watch a lot of TV now.
   4) ....

Jim: I don't go to bed early any more.
   5) ....

Pam: I go jogging now.
   6) ....

7 Reader's Corner

1 Read the article and answer the questions below. Then, explain the words in bold.

THE ANASAZI INDIANS

The Anasazi Indians lived in the USA over 1000 years ago. Their houses were in the side of a "mesa" – a rock in the shape of a high, flat table. The buildings looked like large blocks of flats and there were over 200 rooms. There were windows in the houses, but no doors. To get into their homes, the Anasazi climbed a **ladder** and jumped through a hole in the **roof**! This was also a way of keeping out unwelcome visitors. The Anasazi were farmers. They lived at the **bottom** of the mesa, but farmed on top of it. The area where they lived is called Mesa Verde (Spanish for "green table"). To get up and down the mesa, they made small holes in the rock for their **toes** and **fingers**!

The Anasazi grew corn and beans. They kept turkeys to eat and used the feathers to make their blankets and clothes warmer. The women made beautiful **pots** and **baskets** for carrying things. Even the children had jobs: they helped **grind** the corn and looked after the younger children.

The Anasazi disappeared very suddenly and no one knows exactly what happened to them – perhaps they left their village to look for food and water, or perhaps they were killed by other Native Americans.

Today, you can visit the Anasazi **ruins** at Mesa Verde National Park and imagine what a colourful and interesting life the Anasazi Indians lived.

1. Where did the Anasazi build their homes?
2. What was unusual about their houses?
3. Which crops did they grow?
4. What did they use turkeys for?
5. What did the women do?
6. What did the children do?
7. What happened to the Anasazi?
8. Where can you see the ruins of the Anasazi homes?

2 Read the text again and make notes under the following headings. Then, talk about the Anasazi Indians.

- homes • food • jobs • reasons why they disappeared

3 Portfolio: How many Native Americans tribes do you know? Find information about as many as you can and write a short paragraph about them. Include: homes, food, jobs, things they made, etc.

Progress Check

Vocabulary & Grammar

A Circle the correct item.

1. I was born .... 1st March.
   A in   B at   C on

2. I .... to ride a bike when I was young.
   A used   B use   C am used

3. A(n) .... is a thin stick with a pointed end.
   A bow   B arrow   C drum

4. We visited our aunt .... the weekend.
   A on   B in   C at

5. Michelle Pfeiffer is a famous ....
   A singer   B actress   C writer

6. Alan didn't .... a take-away meal yesterday.
   A order   B ordered   C orders

7. Jo goes to work .... 9:00.
   A on   B at   C in

8. .... TV last night?
   A Do you watch
   B Did you watch
   C Are you watching

9. A .... looks after sheep.
   A shepherd   B wizard   C vet

10. They .... their trip a week ago.
    A plan   B planned   C plans

11. My dad .... to tell me wonderful stories.
    A use   B uses   C used

12. .... live in the sea and on land.
    A Deer   B Buffalo   C Seals

13. I used to .... in a small house, but now I live in a large one.
    A live   B living   C lives

14. The Smiths moved to their new house .... 1987.
    A on   B in   C at

15. "The Northerners" is my favourite ....
    A soap opera   B comedy   C film

16. How .... your first day at work?
    A were   B wasn't   C was

17. The Cheyenne used to play the ....
    A guitar   B violin   C drums

18. David asked Julie to marry him .... Valentine's Day.
    A on   B in   C at

19. Pam was born .... 22nd March.
    A at   B on   C in

20. The Inuit lived in ....
    A igloos   B tepees   C villas

Communication

B Complete the exchanges.

a No, it was a complete disaster!
b I visited my cousins.
c Really hectic!
d Did you do anything special over the weekend?
e What about you?

1. A: How was your weekend?
   B: ....
   Shopping, cooking – tennis on Sunday.

2. A: ....
   B: Not bad. I just stayed at home.

3. A: Did you have a nice weekend, Ben?
   B: ....

4. A: ....
   B: Not really. I studied for my test.

5. A: What did you do at the weekend, Ralph?
   B: ....

Total: _____
25x4   100 marks

61

8a Once upon the Earth ...

Vocabulary Practice

1 Match the definitions with the correct kind of animal.

1 They haven't got wings. They lay eggs. ....
2 They have got feathers, two legs and two wings. They can fly. ....
3 They have got fins and tails. They live in water. ....
4 They have babies and feed their young with milk. ....

a birds
b mammals
c fish
d reptiles

2 Write the opposites.

1 a long tail ≠ a *short* tail
2 a small head ≠ a .... head
3 a large body ≠ a .... body
4 short legs ≠ .... legs
5 short hair ≠ .... hair
6 small wings ≠ .... wings
7 big eyes ≠ .... eyes
8 a thick neck ≠ a .... neck

3 Look at the notes, then talk about each animal, as in the example.

Name: Tasmanian Wolf
Type of Animal: Mammal
Features: short ears/legs, a long tail, stripes on its back, pouch to carry its young
Could: hunt at night

Name: Giant Moa
Type of Animal: Bird
Features: small head, big eyes, long neck/legs, wings
Could: run fast
Couldn't: fly

Trivia Time!

Read and choose.

- Which of the following animals can change colour?
  A Chameleon
  B Turtle
  C Cobra

- What was the name of Napoleon's horse?
  A Bucephalus
  B Marengo
  C Pegasus

- The name 'dinosaur' comes from two Greek words and it means ...
  A terrible lizard.
  B cute lizard.
  C dynamic lizard.

The Tasmanian Wolf was a mammal. It had short ears and legs ...

Animal hall of fame

Vocabulary Practice

1 a. Read the text and fill in the gaps with words from the list.

- astronauts • called • flight • loveable • died • space • nature

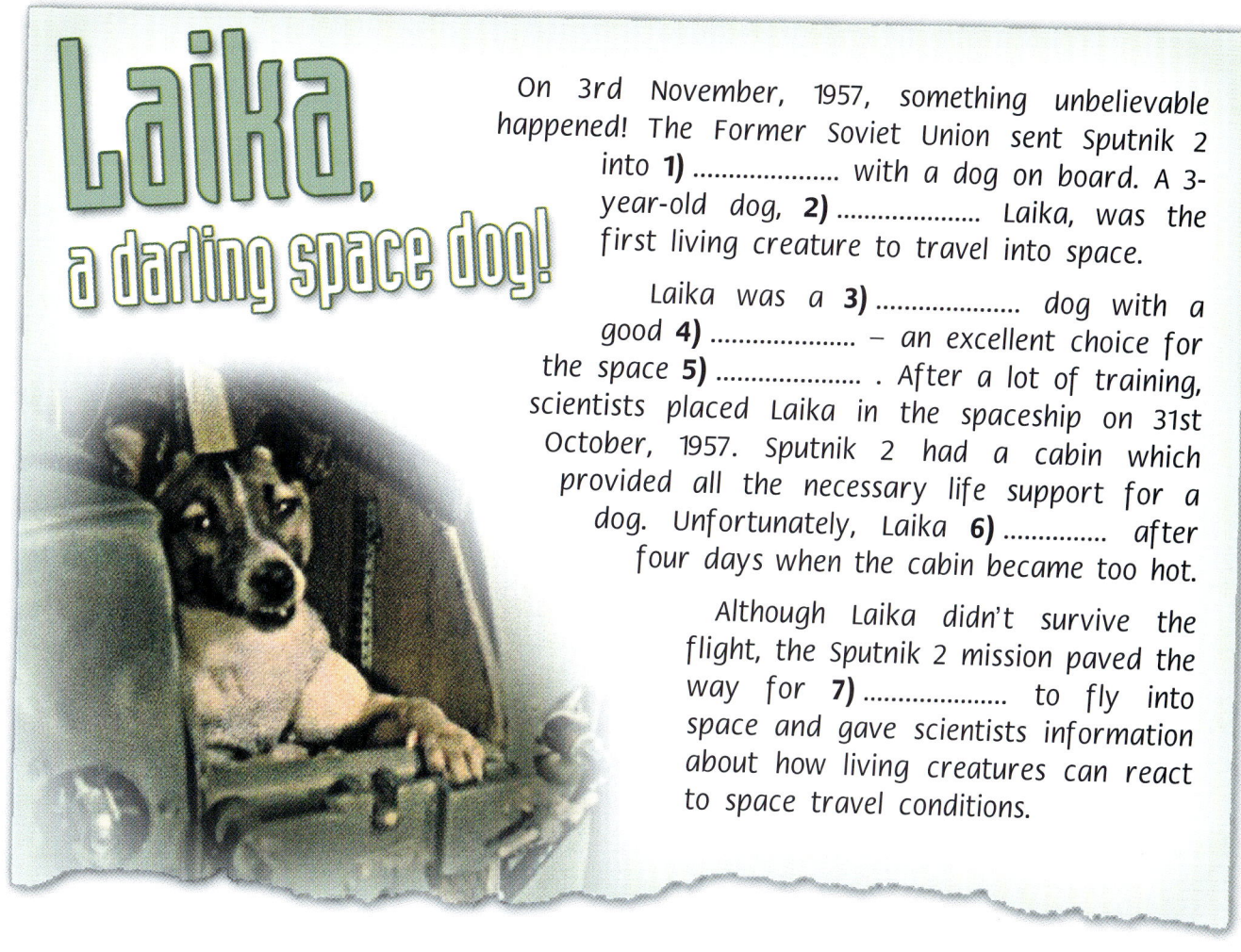

Laika, a darling space dog!

On 3rd November, 1957, something unbelievable happened! The Former Soviet Union sent Sputnik 2 into **1)** .... with a dog on board. A 3-year-old dog, **2)** .... Laika, was the first living creature to travel into space.

Laika was a **3)** .... dog with a good **4)** .... – an excellent choice for the space **5)** .... After a lot of training, scientists placed Laika in the spaceship on 31st October, 1957. Sputnik 2 had a cabin which provided all the necessary life support for a dog. Unfortunately, Laika **6)** .... after four days when the cabin became too hot.

Although Laika didn't survive the flight, the Sputnik 2 mission paved the way for **7)** .... to fly into space and gave scientists information about how living creatures can react to space travel conditions.

b. Read the text again and complete the sentences. Do not use more than three words.

1 The Former Soviet Union sent Sputnik 2 .... in 1957.
2 Laika was the first .... to travel into space.
3 Sputnik 2 provided all the necessary .... for a dog.
4 Laika .... the flight. She died when the cabin became too hot.

2 a. Match the words to their synonyms.

1 small   a clever
2 brave   b cute
3 smart   c little
4 loveable   d easy
5 perfect   e courageous
6 simple   f best

b. Make sentences with the adjectives in the first column.

1 *I live in a small flat.*
2 ....
3 ....
4 ....
5 ....
6 ....

8c Storyline

Listening & Speaking

1 🎧 Listen to Janet talking to her friend, Lucy, about an embarrassing moment. For questions 1-5, circle the correct answer A, B or C.

1 When did the story happen?
  A in the morning
  B at night
  C in the afternoon

2 Where was Janet?
  A in a bank
  B at a supermarket
  C in a department store

3 What did Janet want to buy?
  A clothes
  B shoes
  C food

4 What did Janet forget to take with her?
  A her mobile phone
  B her purse
  C her bag

5 How did Janet feel?
  A happy
  B angry
  C embarrassed

2 You had a nasty/funny experience. Tell your friend:

- what happened
- when/where it happened
- how you felt

Everyday English

3 Circle the correct response.

1 A: I forgot to take my credit card with me.
  B: a I don't believe it!
     b That's wonderful!

2 A: Sam failed his driving test again.
  B: a You're joking!
     b That's great!

3 A: Did you know that Marie Curie won two Nobel Prizes, one for Physics and one for Chemistry?
  B: a Really? I didn't know that!
     b I'm not so sure!

4 A: Tony gave me a diamond ring as a present for our wedding anniversary.
  B: a Oh, no!
     b Wow!

5 A: Something really strange happened to me yesterday!
  B: a Did it? What?
     b Oh, it's terrible!

6 A: Did you know that as a child Bill Gates used to spend his time writing programmes and learning all about computers?
  B: a It's fantastic!
     b Really? I'm not surprised!

4 Use the phrases to respond to the people's news.

- Never! • Wow! • Did it? • Really?
- I didn't know that! • You're joking, surely!

1 A: Peter proposed to me yesterday!
  B: ....

2 A: They cancelled the performance.
  B: ....

3 A: I left my keys at home!
  B: ....

4 A: Something really embarrassing happened to me yesterday!
  B: ....

5 A: I got the job!
  B: ....

6 A: Did you know that Nelson Mandela was a shepherd when he was five years old?
  B: ....

Writing 8d

A

1) *Last* week, I decided to eat my lunch in the park because it was a nice, sunny day. I took my sandwich and sat on a bench by the pond.
   Two minutes 2) ...., a big brown dog appeared and jumped on the bench beside me. I gave it a piece of my sandwich 3) .... looked around for its owner. I couldn't see anyone, 4) .... I looked on the dog's collar for an address. 5) ...., I knew the street where the dog lived, so I took it home.
   6) .... I knocked on the door, I got a big surprise. Standing in front of me was Willie Robbins, my favourite singer! He was really pleased to see his dog again and gave me a free ticket for his concert.
   7) ...., I went to see him sing and I sat in the front row. He came on stage and smiled at me, then said 'This song is for my good friend, Debra. It's called 'Rescue me'! It was the best moment of my life!

A story

1 a. Read the rubric, look at the pictures and answer the questions.

Write a story for a magazine competition with the title: The best moment of my life.

1 What do you think the story is about?
2 Who is the story about?
3 What happened?

b. Now, read the story and check your answers.

2 Read the story again and complete. Use: *last, that evening, and, later, when, so, luckily*.

3 Read the story again and answer the questions.

1 When/Where did the story take place?
2 Where did Debra sit to eat her sandwich?
3 What jumped on the bench beside her?
4 What did Debra do then?
5 Why did she look on the dog's collar?
6 What did she do with the dog?
7 Who opened the door?
8 What did he give Debra?
9 Where did she go that evening?
10 What song did Willie Robbins sing?
11 How did Debra feel?

4 a. Think about the best moment of your life and answer the questions.

The Best Moment of My Life

Paragraph 1 – When/Where did it happen? Who were you with?

Paragraph 2 – How did it start?

Paragraph 3 – What happened then?

Paragraph 4 – What happened at the end? How did you feel?

b. Portfolio: Use your ideas from Ex. 4a and the model from Ex. 1b to write a story for a magazine competition about *The best moment of your life*.

65

8 Grammar in Use

1 In pairs, ask and answer, as in the example.

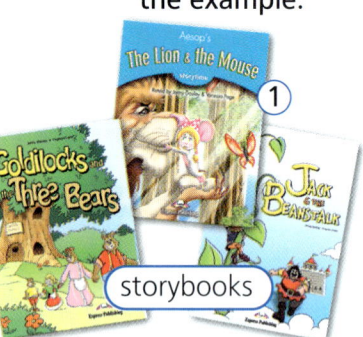

1. storybooks
2. teddy bear
3. camera
4. bike
5. guitar
6. watch
7. pet

A: Did you have storybooks when you were six years old?
B: Yes, I did.

2 Mrs Edwards is 70 years old. What could she do when she was young but can't do now? Make sentences using the prompts below, as in the example.

1. eat spicy food
2. dance all night
3. ski
4. lift heavy things
5. go for long walks

1 *Mrs Edwards could eat spicy food when she was young, but she can't now.*

3 Write the *past simple* of the following verbs. Then, use six of the verbs to make sentences.

1. tell — *told*
2. have — ....
3. get — ....
4. bring — ....
5. write — ....
6. come — ....
7. eat — ....
8. go — ....

4 Put the verbs in brackets into the *Past Simple*.

1. A: Where *did you go* (you/go) last summer, Paul?
   B: I .... (go) to Paris with friends.

2. A: What .... (she/have) for breakfast?
   B: She .... (not/eat) anything, she just .... (drink) some orange juice.

3. A: What .... (be) that noise?
   B: I .... (not/hear) anything.

4. A: .... (you/go) shopping yesterday?
   B: No, I .... (not/have) time.

5. A: What .... (you/do) last weekend?
   B: I .... (drive) to the beach with my friends and .... (spend) all day there.

6. A: What .... (Sheila/buy) yesterday?
   B: She .... (buy) a new dress to wear to the party on Saturday.

5 Form the questions, then answer them about yourself.

1. When/you/send/e-mail/your friend?
   When did you send an e-mail to your friend?
2. What/you/buy/yesterday?
   ....
3. How/you/meet/your best friend?
   ....
4. What/you/watch/TV/yesterday evening?
   ....
5. Where/you/go/for your holiday?
   ....
6. When/you/last/eat/a restaurant?
   ....

6 Ask and answer, as in the example.

- watch a film
- go shopping
- meet your friends
- play computer games
- eat cornflakes for breakfast
- visit your grandfather
- buy a pair of trainers
- study for a test

S1: Did you watch a film yesterday?
S2: Yes, I did. Did you go shopping yesterday?
S3: No, I didn't. Did you …

7 Put the verbs into the *past simple*, then match the questions to the answers, as in the example.

Quiz

1	D	Which city *held* (hold) the Olympic Games in 2004?
2		Who .... (write) "Romeo and Juliet"?
3		Who .... (build) the Parthenon?
4		Who first .... (fly) into space?
5		Who .... (invent) the telephone?
6		Who .... (win) a Nobel Prize in Physics?
7		Who .... (lose) the battle of Waterloo?
8		Who .... (compose) nine symphonies?

- A Beethoven
- B Napoleon
- C Alexander Graham Bell
- D Athens
- E Albert Einstein
- F Yuri Gagarin
- G Ictinus and Callicrates
- H William Shakespeare

8 Write true sentences about yourself using the time expressions in the list below.

- two months ago • last night • yesterday
- in 2002 • last summer • last Sunday

1 *I went to the theatre two months ago.*
2 ....
3 ....
4 ....
5 ....
6 ....

9 Read and match.

1	d	As Pat got off the train,
2		She looked around,
3		He fell asleep
4		Tony heard a loud explosion.

a as soon as he closed his eyes.
b Suddenly, the train stopped.
c then put the envelope in her pocket.
d she saw Phil waiting for her.

10 Fill in the gaps with *then*, *as*, *as soon as*, *suddenly*.

1 Karen was out in the back garden. *Suddenly*, she smelled something burning.
2 He put on his coat and .... he went outside.
3 .... she turned on the TV, the doorbell rang.
4 I watched her .... she brushed her hair.
5 .... he got home, she started making dinner.
6 We saw the smoke .... we turned into Green Street.
7 She brushed her teeth and .... she went to bed.
8 Julie was in the living room. ...., she heard a strange noise.

8 Reader's Corner

1 What was the name of the first man to orbit Earth? Where was he from?

2 Read and say why the following dates are important: *9th March, 1934; 12th April, 1961; 27th March, 1968.*

A Russian Hero

Yuri Gagarin was born near Moscow, Russia on the 9th of March, 1934. He joined the Soviet Air Force in 1955 and started training as a cosmonaut in 1959.

On 12th April, 1961, Yuri Gagarin became the first human to orbit Earth. The name of his spacecraft was Vostok 1. It had two sections: one for Yuri and one for supplies such as water and oxygen.

Vostok 1's flight lasted 108 minutes. Yuri did not land in the spacecraft. He ejected and landed by parachute!

Sadly, Yuri Gagarin was killed in a plane crash on 27th March, 1968, before he could travel into space a second time. There is a crater on the moon that is named after this great Russian hero.

3 Read again and fill in the flight details. Then, talk about Yuri Gagarin.

Name of spaceship: ....
Name of cosmonaut: ....
Number of sections: ....
Supplies: ....
Length of flight: ....
Method of landing: ....

Over to you!

4 **Portfolio:** Find information about the *Apollo 11* flight to the moon and write a factfile with the flight details.

Name of spaceship: *Apollo 11*
Name of astronauts: ....
Number of sections: ....
Supplies: ....
Length of flight: ....
Method of landing: ....

Progress Check

Vocabulary & Grammar

A Circle the correct item.

1. Elephant Birds are .... There aren't any alive today.
   A extinct   B small   C heavy

2. These tools have sharp ...., so be careful.
   A teeth   B blades   C fins

3. Snakes and crocodiles are ....
   A fish   B mammals   C reptiles

4. Brad .... me a ring for my birthday.
   A gives   B gave   C is giving

5. .... to Beth's party last night?
   A Did you go   B Do you go
   C Are you going

6. Plesiosaurus had four ....
   A wings   B flippers   C fins

7. James .... travelling when he was young.
   A enjoyed   B enjoy   C enjoys

8. .... Pete got his results, he called me.
   A As soon as   B Suddenly   C Then

9. When Mary .... Rob's story, she started laughing.
   A hear   B heard   C hears

10. .... have babies and feed them with milk.
    A Mammals   B Birds   C Reptiles

11. ...., she saw a snake in front of her.
    A Suddenly   B Before   C As

12. He made his first space .... last October.
    A travel   B walk   C flight

13. John didn't .... to the concert last night.
    A go   B went   C goes

14. We came to school an hour ....
    A last   B yesterday   C ago

15. "Did you go to the gym yesterday?" "Yes, I ...."
    A go   B went   C did

16. Sean .... to Spain last summer.
    A reached   B went   C sent

17. Plesiosaurus was from three to eighteen metres ....
    A big   B large   C long

18. I .... eat the cake. Liz ate it.
    A don't   B didn't   C doesn't

19. Jules Verne .... many exciting stories.
    A told   B wrote   C said

20. Dunkleosteus .... swim very fast.
    A did   B can   C could

Communication

B Complete the exchanges.

a Really! I didn't know that!
b Wow!
c Something really funny happened to me yesterday!
d Brian got married yesterday.
e I don't believe it!

1. A: ....
   B: Did it? What?

2. A: I left the tickets at home!
   B: ....

3. A: Jill gave me a gold watch as a present.
   B: ....

4. A: Walt Disney had pet field mice!
   B: ....

5. A: ....
   B: Are you sure?

(Total: ——— / 25x4   100 marks)

9a Tomorrow's world

Vocabulary Practice

1 a. Look at the picture and number the sentences.

- [1] Our air cars will fly you all over the city!
- [ ] The most intelligent kitchens you've ever seen!
- [ ] We will take you on a virtual tour that will make your head spin!
- [ ] Keep in the pink all day – wear our 'Clothes to suit your mood' range!
- [ ] A live-in robot is a man's best friend!

b. What will life be like in the future? Say.

1 *We will fly around in air cars.*

2 Match the phrases. Then use them to complete the sentences.

1	c	solar	a	pills
2		space	b	holidays
3		intelligent	c	energy
4		nutrition	d	stations
5		virtual	e	kitchens

1 It's better to use *solar energy* instead of petrol.
2 People won't go on real holidays, but on ....
3 Food will become a thing of the past: everyone will take .... instead.
4 .... will be able to order and prepare food.
5 Holidays of the future will be different: we'll be able to go on holiday at ....

Everyday English

3 Will life be better or worse in the future? Talk with your friend.

Giving an opinion
- I think …
- I'm sure …
- In my opinion, …

Agreeing
I think you're right.
I like the sound of that.

Disagreeing
Oh, I don't agree.
Do you really think so?
No way!
I don't think so.

1 The ice at the North and South Poles will melt.
2 A lot of cities will be under water.
3 Our planet will get colder and we'll all go to live on the moon.
4 There will be robots in all the workplaces.
5 Our working day will only be four hours.
6 A pill will stop people getting fat.

A: *I think the ice at the North and South Poles will melt!*
B: *I think you're right!*

Action-packed! 9b

Vocabulary Practice

1 Look at the pictures and complete the crossword puzzle.

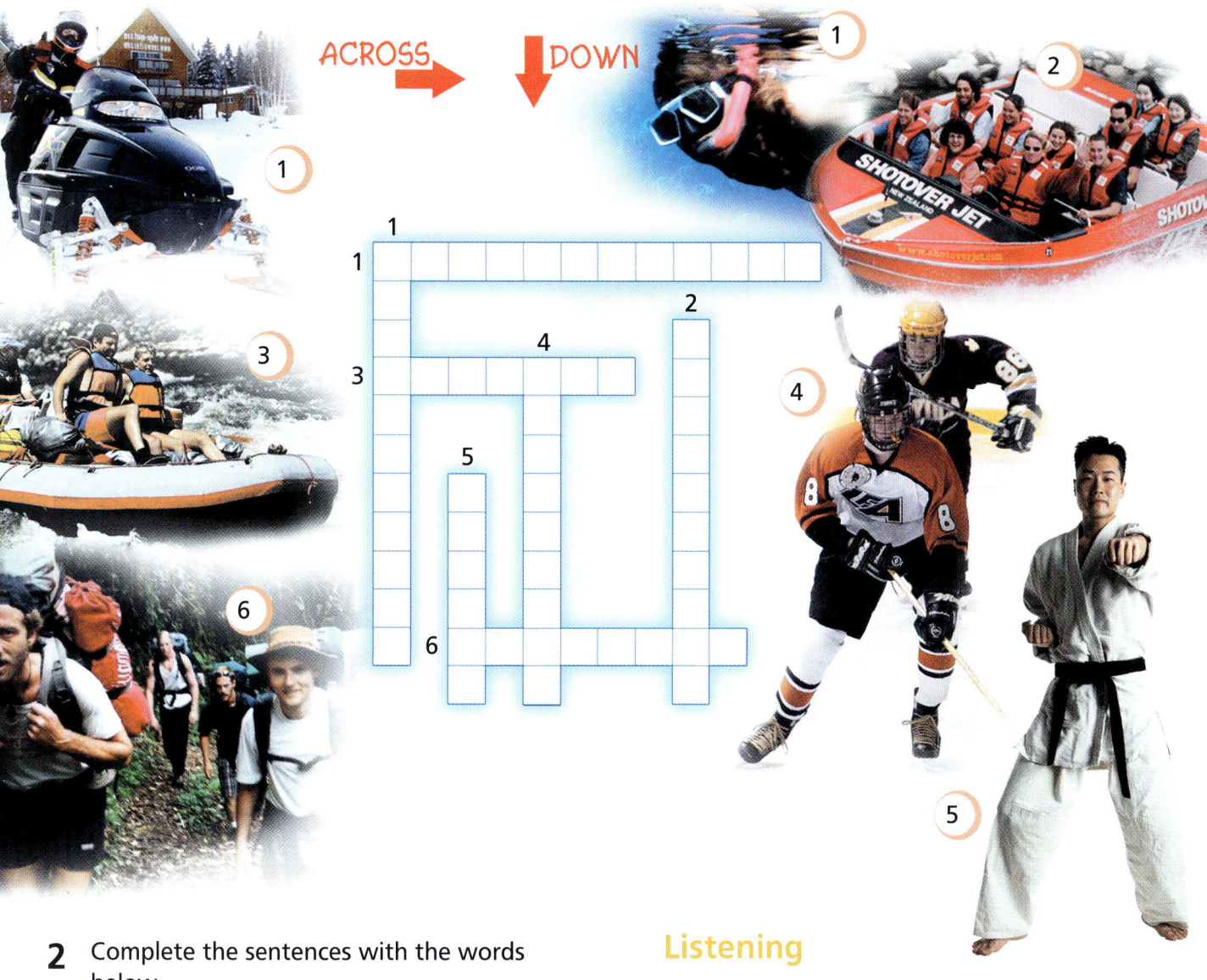

ACROSS → DOWN ↓

2 Complete the sentences with the words below.

- surfing • opportunity • exciting • region
- expedition • tribe • tough

1 The Cheyenne were a *tribe* of Native Americans.
2 They had a(n) .... time when they went on safari.
3 Going to Italy will give me the .... to speak Italian.
4 Provence is a well known .... of France.
5 He likes to go where there are big waves because he loves ....
6 The exam was ...., but I think I've passed it.
7 You need to be fit to go on a(n) .... to the North Pole.

Listening

3 🎧 Listen and complete.

Name: Ellie 1 ....

Age: 2 ....

Interests: music, 3 ....

Preferred country: 4 ....

Available from: 5 20th ....

71

9c Making plans

Vocabulary Practice

1 Read and write the word.

1 You need one of these to play tennis with.
r <u>a c k e t</u>
2 This protects your head when you're cycling.
h _ _ _ _ _ _
3 You should wear one of these when you do water sports.
l _ _ _ _ _ _ _ _ _
4 These help you swim faster.
f _ _ _ _ _ _ _
5 You need these when you're on the slopes.
s _ _ _
6 These will help you see under water.
g _ _ _ _ _ _
7 You need one of these to ride the big waves.
s _ _ _ _ _ _ _ _
8 This holds all your clothes, food, etc. when you go travelling.
r _ _ _ _ _ _ _

Everyday English

2 Read and choose.

1 A: We can all stay out until late!
B: a What time is it?
(b) That's perfect!
c Where's that?

2 A: Are you doing anything tonight?
B: a That sounds nice.
b Yes, I'd love to.
c I'm not sure. Why?

3 A: Do you fancy going for a meal?
B: a It's not my type.
b What have you got in mind?
c In a minute.

4 A: Let's go swimming!
B: a I'll give you a ring.
b I'm afraid I can't.
c No, I'm not.

3 In pairs, use the phrases and the prompts to ask and answer, as in the example.

• go to the theatre • play football • watch a film • go for coffee • go shopping

Column A
- Do you fancy …?
- How about …?
- Why don't we …?
- Let's …!
- Are you doing anything at the weekend?

Column B
- That's a brilliant idea!
- That's fine by me.
- Sure, why not?
- I'm afraid I can't.
- Thanks, but I can't.

A: Let's go to the theatre.
B: That's a brilliant idea!

Reading

4 Read and complete the dialogue. Then, make notes and read it out.

Judy: Ben, did you put the tent in the car?
Ben: 1) ....
Judy: What time is Phil coming round with the sleeping bags?
Ben: 2) ....
Judy: I'm going to make something to eat for the journey. What do you fancy?
Ben: 3) ....
Judy: OK. I'll take some fruit with us as well.
Ben: 4) ....
Judy: In about half an hour.
Ben: 5) ....
Judy: Oh, Ben!

A I'll just have some sandwiches … oh – and can you make some coffee?
B Not yet. I'll do it in a minute.
C Good idea. When will you be ready to leave?
D Right … I'll ring Phil and put the tent in the car. Er … Judy, have you seen my keys?
E I'm not sure. I'll give him a ring.

72

Writing 9d

A letter of invitation

> **Plan**
>
> **Paragraph 1:** reasons for writing, when the invitation is for
> **Paragraph 2:** details about activities (venues, people involved, etc.)
> **Paragraph 3:** closing remarks

1 Use the plan above to put the paragraphs in the correct order.

A I think it will be a good weekend so I hope you can make it. Write and let me know – it will be great to see you again.
Love,
Matthew

B Dear Angela,
I'm writing to find out about your plans for next weekend. Do you fancy coming to stay? It will be a good opportunity to catch up on all the news and do some fun things together.

C On Friday night, Tiger's Eye are performing at the Roulette, a new venue in town, so I'll get some tickets if you want. Then, on Saturday, Tom and Lisa are going to go rafting, so we could join them. What do you think? On Sunday morning, my football team is playing at Fuller's Stadium and after that we're all coming round to my place for a barbecue.

2 Read the letter again and answer the questions.

1 Who's writing the letter? Who's the letter to?
2 When is the invitation for?
3 Where can they go on Friday night?
4 Who can they join on Saturday?
5 What can they do on Sunday morning?

3 Read the extracts below. Which are *Opening Remarks*? Which are *Closing Remarks*?

A I'd love to see you again. It will be great to catch up on all the news!
See you soon.

B Hi!
How are you? Are you busy next weekend?

C Dear Mike,
I hope all is well with you. What are you doing next Saturday?

D We'll have a great time, I'm sure! I hope you'll be able to join in all the fun!
Write and let me know.
Kisses,

4 Portfolio: Write a letter to a friend inviting him/her for the weekend. Tell him/her what activities you can do together. Use the plan and the model in Ex. 1 to help you.

73

9 Grammar in Use

1 Look, read and write sentences.

1 she/take dog for walk
She is going to take the dog for a walk.

2 He/be late for work
....

3 they/play golf
....

4 they/have dinner
....

5 he/buy new jumper
....

6 they/go fishing
....

2 Bradley is getting ready to go to London for the weekend. What is he going to do there? Look, read and put a tick (✓) or a cross (✗). Then, say.

1 He's going to stay at a hotel. ✓
2 He's going to go by train. ✗
3 He's going to go on a tour of London. ☐
4 He's going to take photos. ☐
5 He's going to go to the cinema. ☐
6 He's going to meet his sister. ☐

Bradley is going to stay at a hotel. He isn't going to go by train. He's going to go …

3 Look at the information about Helen and John's holidays. Ask and answer, as in the example.

Where?	Paris
How/travel?	Eurostar
Where/stay?	hotel
How long/stay?	10 days
What/do?	sightseeing

A: Where are they going to go?
B: They are going to go to Paris.

4 Read and match.

1	e	Is Mick coming over tomorrow?
2		There isn't any shampoo left.
3		These potatoes are cold!
4		Did you pay the phone bill?
5		Is there a good film on tonight?
6		They're bringing the new fridge in the morning.

a Are they? I'll put them in the microwave.
b Oh, I forgot! I'll do it first thing in the morning.
c I'm not sure. I'll look in the TV guide.
d OK. I'll make sure I'm in.
e I don't know. I'll ring him and find out.
f I'll get some while I'm at the supermarket.

74

5 Look at Susan's agenda. Then, ask and answer questions, as in the example.

```
Mon:
    start new job

Tues:
    visit parents

Wed:
    go swimming

Thurs:
    start ballet classes

Fri:
    study for the exams
```

1 (start new job/Wednesday)
   A: *Is she starting her new job on Wednesday?*
   B: *No she isn't. She is starting her new job on Monday.*

2 (visit parents/Friday)
   A: .... ?
   B: ....

3 (go swimming/Tuesday)
   A: .... ?
   B: ....

4 (study for exams/Thursday)
   A: .... ?
   B: ....

6 Answer the questions about yourself using *I think*, *perhaps*, *probably*, as in the example.

1 Where will you go on Saturday night?
   I think I'll go to the cinema.
2 What will you do at Christmas?
   ....
3 Where will you be at 9:00 tomorrow?
   ....
4 What will you do on your birthday?
   ....
5 When will you go on holiday?
   ....
6 Who will you go with?
   ....

7 Use *will* or *won't* to make predictions about the future, as in the example.

1 In the future people *will* live longer.
2 People .... do any housework. A robot will do it for them.
3 People .... use petrol. They will use solar energy.
4 Clothes .... change colour to suit our mood.
5 There .... be a pill to keep people slim.
6 Fridges .... order everything we need.

8 Fill in the gaps with *will* or *be going to*.

1 Janet is going to town.
   She *is going to* buy a new coat.
2 A: I can't reach the coffee jar.
   B: Don't worry. I .... get it for you.
3 A: I'm hungry!
   B: OK. I .... make you a sandwich.
4 We've got two tickets for the concert. We .... go this evening.
5 Sorry, I can't come out tonight. I .... visit my cousin.
6 A: Kathy's late. I wonder where she is.
   B: I .... call her on her mobile phone.

Trivia Time!

Read and choose.

- Which country is famous for its Highland Games?
  A Spain
  B Russia
  C Scotland

- Which car colour has the most accidents?
  A Yellow
  B Red
  C Black

- Which was the official language of England for over 600 years?
  A French
  B Gaelic
  C German

9 Reader's Corner

1 Explain the difference between *fresh*, *frozen* and *canned food*. What are *proteins*, *vitamins* and *minerals*?

2 Read the title. What do you think we will eat in the future? Tell the class. Then, read the article and check your guesses.

Food for the Future

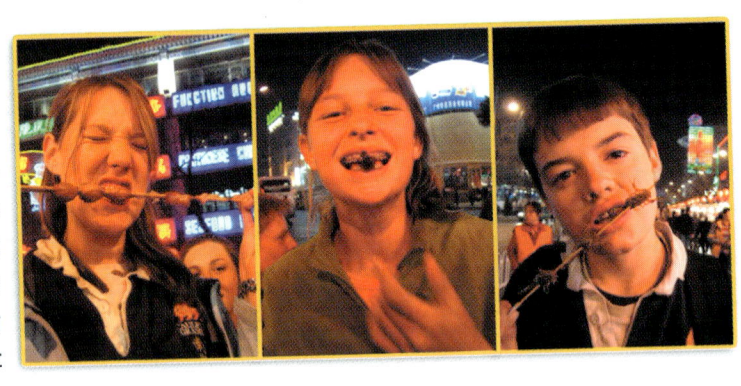

When you think of the type of food that there will be in thirty years' time, what do you imagine? A plate of pills? Compact meals like aeroplane food? Meal-making computers? Think again ... insects are the food of the future! It is very likely that within the next ten years, you will be able to buy fresh, canned or frozen insects at your local supermarket!

You'll be surprised to hear that insects are actually very good for you – they contain as much protein as chicken or beef, as well as vitamins and minerals. In some countries in the world, they plant crops for the insects that eat the crops: it's the insects they want, not the crops! In years to come, our planet won't have enough food to feed cows and other animals, so insects will become a normal part of our meals!

So, the next time you find a caterpillar in your salad, don't scream! Just stop to think a minute. Maybe in the future, caterpillars will be your favourite dish ... yummy!

3 Read the article again and choose.

1. You will be able to buy fresh, canned or frozen insects in the future.
   A Right   B Wrong   C Doesn't Say

2. Insects contain protein, vitamins and minerals.
   A Right   B Wrong   C Doesn't Say

3. In Africa, they plant crops because they want the insects.
   A Right   B Wrong   C Doesn't Say

4. We will eat a lot of meat from animals in the future.
   A Right   B Wrong   C Doesn't Say

5. There will be farms for insects in the future.
   A Right   B Wrong   C Doesn't Say

4 You work for a company called *Tasty Insects*. Explain to a customer why insects are the food of the future. Use ideas from the article.

5 Portfolio: You work for an advertising company. Design a poster for a campaign in favour of insects.

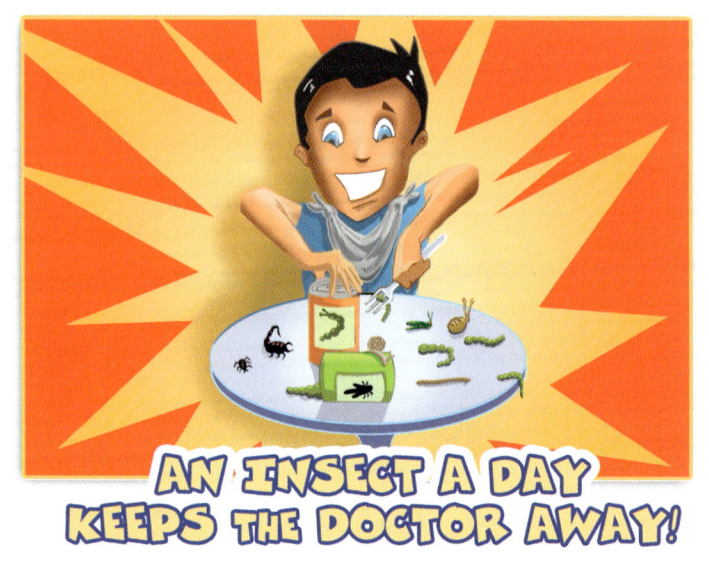

AN INSECT A DAY KEEPS THE DOCTOR AWAY!

Progress Check

Vocabulary & Grammar

A Circle the correct item.

1 In the future, people .... use money.
 A aren't B won't C don't

2 We will have .... that will fly in the air.
 A house B machine C cars

3 She .... to London tomorrow night.
 A will fly B is flying C flew

4 She usually goes .... at the weekend.
 A surfing B karate
 C water sports

5 Our daily .... will change a great deal.
 A world B job C routine

6 Are you going to .... our club?
 A join B joining C joined

7 I think I .... some sandwiches for the trip.
 A will make B am going to make
 C make

8 In a few years, cars will use .... energy instead of petrol.
 A wind B solar C water

9 Going on holiday to China was the .... of a lifetime.
 A research B chance C skill

10 He is swimming with his new ....
 A flippers B skis C lifejacket

11 He needs a new .... for the tennis match on Tuesday.
 A helmet B goggles C racket

12 Dad's at the newsagent's. He .... a newspaper.
 A bought B is going to buy
 C buys

13 Where .... from 20th to 30th of June?
 A she will be B is she going to be
 C is she

14 We can go .... in the mountains.
 A surfing B rafting C trekking

15 "The CD player isn't working." "I know; I .... it later."
 A fix B fixing
 C am going to fix

16 There will be space station .... in the future.
 A vacations B computers
 C houses

17 I .... you a ring at about seven tonight.
 A am giving B will give C give

18 Clothes will change colour to .... your mood.
 A hold B suit C keep

19 "Bye. I .... you when I get back!"
 A am going B will see
 C am seeing

20 She takes vitamin .... every day to stay healthy.
 A food B plates C pills

Communication

B Complete the exchanges.

 a Mm, I'm not sure.
 b Would you like to go for a pizza?
 c Sorry, I can't.
 d Are you doing anything tonight?
 e That sounds great!

1 A: ....
 B: Yes, I'd love to.

2 A: How about going to the cinema?
 B: ....
 I think I'll just watch a DVD at home.

3 A: Let's play football!
 B: .... I'll bring my new ball.

4 A: Shall we go surfing?
 B: .... I have to study.

5 A: ....
 B: Yes, I've arranged to meet Paul.

(Total: _____)
(25x4 100 marks)

77

10a On your travels

Vocabulary Practice

1 Label the objects.

- pool • mobile phone • alarm clock • money • gum

1 mobile phone
2 ....
3 ....
4 ....
5 ....

2 Match the phrases. Then, use them to complete the sentences.

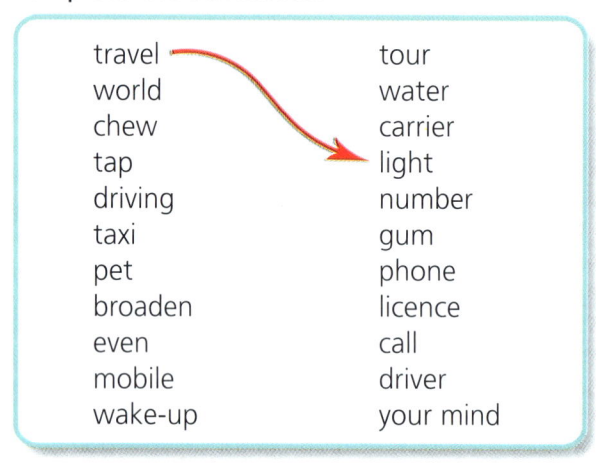

travel	tour
world	water
chew	carrier
tap	light
driving	number
taxi	gum
pet	phone
broaden	licence
even	call
mobile	driver
wake-up	your mind

1 To rent a car, you must have your .... with you.
2 I don't think it's safe to drink the .... Buy some bottled water instead.
3 I'm not taking a lot of clothes with me; I'll .... this time.
4 You mustn't .... when you talk to people. It's rude.
5 You can take the dog with you as long as it's in a ....
6 While you are on a plane, you must switch off your ....
7 2, 4, 6 and 8 are ....
8 The band will go on a .... They will play in about fifteen different countries.
9 'I forgot to bring my alarm clock with me.' 'Don't worry. We can ask for a ....'

10 In my country, a .... mustn't carry more than four passengers.
11 Travelling can .... It's a good way to understand and accept other people's beliefs and customs.

3 Circle the odd word out.

1 city, neon lights, train, towels
2 train, airport, plane, taxi
3 cashier, host, shop, counter
4 pet, flight, plane, airport
5 taxi driver, waiter, cashier, flower
6 pet, alarm clock, pet carrier, dog

4 Fill in the correct word from the list.

- fill up • tip • chew • punctual • take off
- host • sole • cashier

1 I usually *tip* the waiter because I like the service here.
2 Jenny is very .... She's always on time.
3 This meat is so tough, I can't .... it!
4 Our .... welcomed us warmly into his house.
5 The robber shouted at the .... to put the money in a bag.
6 Tom burnt the .... of his foot.
7 My glass is empty. Can you .... it ...., please?
8 In Japan, you should .... your shoes .... as you enter the house.

Well-travelled! 10b

Vocabulary Practice

1 Look and complete the words.

1. j..................
2. m..................
3. w..................
4. l..................
5. b..................
6. f..................
7. r..................
8. c..................

Reading

2 a. Fill in the gaps with the words below:

- volcano • luau • beaches • surfed • palm

Dear Kelly,

It's fantastic here in Hawaii! We're having a great time. You should see all the sandy 1) .... and beautiful 2) .... trees. Amazing! We've done lots of things so far – we've been to a 3) .... and we've 4) .... in the Pacific Ocean! Tomorrow, we're going to see Mauna Loa, the world's biggest 5) .... I can't wait!

See you next week.
Love,
Sandra and Pete

Hawaii - 2005 -Hanauma Bay

b. Answer the questions.

1 Where are Sandra and Pete?
....

2 Where have they been?
....

3 What are they going to see tomorrow?
....

4 When are they coming back?
....

79

10c Time for a change!

Listening

1 🎧 Listen and complete questions 1-5.

Marsden Hall Spa

First name: Chris

Surname: 1 ....

Choice of exercise class: 2 ....

Choice of water exercise: 3 ....

Date: 4 Saturday, ...

Cost: 5 £ ....

Speaking

2 You meet a friend from school who you haven't seen for a very long time. Ask him/her about the things that have changed in his/her life over the years.

Everyday English

3 a. Fill in the gaps with the phrases below.

- You've made my day
- I really like your new dress

1) ....!

Thank you! That's very kind of you to say so!

Have you lost weight? You look wonderful!

Thank you! 2) ....!

b. Act out similar dialogues.

Trivia Time!

Read and choose.

- Which country is famous for the traditional dish called Paella?
  A Sweden
  B Spain
  C England

- Which European capital does the river Seine flow through?
  A Paris
  B London
  C Rome

- What is Miami famous for?
  A its waterfall
  B its bridge
  C being a beach resort

80

Writing 10d

A leaflet

1 What do you know about Singapore? Would you like to visit it? Why/Why not?

2 Look at the pictures and match them to the sentences below. Then, read the leaflet and check your answers.

1 *You can find anything you need – and at great prices!* ......
2 *Drinking afternoon tea here was like going back in time!* ......
3 *The selection of food will make you dizzy!* ......
4 *Breakfast with mum and baby was the best part of my trip!* ......
5 *The city at night takes your breath away!* ......

3 Read the leaflet again and fill in the headings.

A Nightlife D Shopping
B Eating Out E Places to Visit
C Accommodation

4 Say three things you would like to do in Singapore.

5 a. Answer the following questions about your town/city.

1 Where can visitors stay? Are there any popular hotels?
2 Which places can they visit?
3 Where can they eat? What kind of food can they try?
4 Where are the best places to shop?
5 Where can they go in the evening?

b. **Portfolio:** You work for a travel agency. Your boss asked you to produce a leaflet for visitors to your town/city. Use your answers from Ex. 5a and the model in Ex. 2 and write the leaflet.

SINGAPORE – THE LION CITY

Singapore, or as some call it, The Lion City, is a city, an island and a country in Asia. It is a bridge between the East and the West and an interesting mixture of cultures.

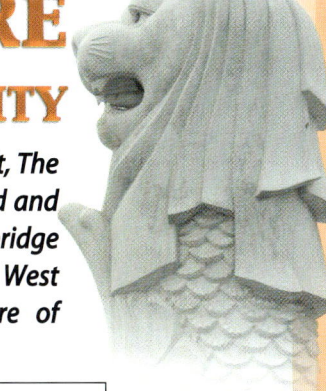

1 ....

Finding a place to stay will be no problem in Singapore. There are many hotels to choose from, including some wonderful five-star hotels such as *The Ritz-Carlton Hotel*, *Shangri-La Hotel* and the most famous of all *Raffles Hotel*.

2 ....

Visit one of Singapore's famous spas or have breakfast with an orangutan at the beautiful Singapore Zoo!

3 ....

Eating out is a delight in Singapore. There are plenty of Indian and Chinese restaurants in the city as well as places that serve international food.

4 ....

A single day will take you from quiet gardens and tea rooms to a busy city centre offering some of the best shopping in the world! *Centerpoint* is the place to go if you are a serious shopper.

5 ....

The Lion City comes alive at night. Party animals roam around the golden triangle of nightspots – *Zouk, Mohammed Sultan Road* and *Boat Quay*. Not a night person? You can always head for the centre and watch a Broadway show.

With its friendly and welcoming people, a visit to Singapore is an experience you'll never forget!

81

10 Grammar in Use

Grammar Practice

1 a. Have you ever stayed in a hotel? Were there any rules? Tell the class.

b. Read and complete the Hotel De La Mer rules. Use *must* or *mustn't*.

Hotel De La Mer

We wish all our guests an enjoyable stay. To ensure everyone's comfort, we would like to remind all visitors to the hotel of the following rules:

- You 1) .... check out by 12 o'clock noon.
- You 2) .... bring pets into the hotel.
- You 3) .... leave your keys at reception.
- You 4) .... play loud music after 11 o'clock.
- You 5) .... report any damage to the hotel manager.
- You 6) .... eat or drink in the reception area.

2 Look at the people's statements and give advice, as in the example.

1. Ann: "I am always late for school."
   (go to bed early)
   You should go to bed early.

2. Jim: "I have a terrible headache."
   (take an aspirin)
   ....

3. Mary: "I have a problem with my eyes."
   (see an optician)
   ....

4. Terry: "It's cold outside."
   (put on a heavy jacket)
   ....

5. Lin: "My dress doesn't fit me."
   (go on a diet)
   ....

3 Choose the correct item.

1. In China, you .... never be late for appointments.
   A mustn't   **B** should   C can

2. In Japan, you .... blow your nose in public.
   A should   B must   C mustn't

3. .... I use your phone?
   A Must   B Should   C Can

4. When in England, you .... say "please" and "thank you".
   A should   B can   C mustn't

5. You .... fasten your seat belt. It's the law.
   A can   B should   C must

6. .... I go camping with my friends at the weekend?
   A Must   B Can   C Should

4 Janet is on holiday in Amsterdam. Talk about what she has already done/hasn't done yet.

- take a boat trip down the Amstel River ✓
- go to the Artis Zoo ✗
- visit the Van Gogh Museum ✓
- visit the Anne Frank House ✗
- take lots of photos ✓
- buy some souvenirs ✓

Janet has already taken a boat trip down the Amstel River.

5 Complete the sentences with the correct verb from the list below, using the *present perfect*.

- not decide • buy • not travel • book • go
- ride • not pack • eat

1. I'm very pleased with my shopping. I *have bought* lots of souvenirs.
2. .... you ever .... on a boat trip on the Seine?
3. Alex and Sylvia still .... where to go for their summer holidays.
4. Kim .... abroad since 1995.
5. I .... never .... a camel.
6. .... you .... a hotel room?
7. I .... Chinese food. It's delicious!
8. Jim .... his things yet.

82

6 Put the verbs in brackets into the *past simple* or the *present perfect*.

1. A: *Have you bought* (you/buy) the plane tickets yet?
   B: Yes, I have. I .... (buy) them yesterday afternoon.
2. A: How was your holiday, Helen?
   B: Great! We .... (have) a fantastic time.
3. A: What's the matter?
   B: I .... (lose) my wallet.
4. A: How long .... (you/be) here?
   B: We .... (be) here for three days. We .... (arrive) on Thursday morning.
5. A: .... (you/ever/break) your arm?
   B: Yes, I .... (break) my arm when I .... (be) thirteen.
6. A: When was the last time you .... (eat) in a Mexican restaurant?
   B: I .... (never/eat) Mexican food.

7 Use the prompts to act out short exchanges.

• do the shopping/already • pay bills/yesterday • move house/yet • redecorate your bedroom/last week • eat frogs' legs/never • visit a museum/last Friday

A: *Have you done the shopping?*
B: *Yes, I've already done it.*

8 Write the superlatives, then try to answer the questions.

1. Which country has *the largest* (large) population in the world?
   A India   B China   C Brazil
2. Which is .... (long) river in the world?
   A the Nile   B the Mississippi   C the Danube
3. Which is .... (high) mountain in the world?
   A Kilimanjaro   B Mount Cook   C Mount Everest
4. Which is .... (small) continent in the world?
   A Europe   B Australia   C Asia
5. Which is .... (hot) place in the world?
   A Cairo   B Cyprus   C Death Valley
6. Where is .... (dry) place in the world?
   A in Chile   B in Japan   C in China

9 Use the prompts below to make sentences, as in the example.

1. Have you met Tom's sister? She's very pretty, isn't she?
   Yes, she's the prettiest girl I've ever met.
2. Have you seen Peter's new car? It's very fast, isn't it?
   ....
3. Have you heard Jessie's joke? It's very funny, isn't it?
   ....
4. Have you tasted my mum's apple pie? It's delicious, isn't it?
   ....
5. Have you met Ron's cousin? He's very handsome, isn't he?
   ....

10 Complete the questions, then answer them.

1. Who is *the best* (good) actor in your country?
2. What is .... (boring) subject at school?
3. What is .... (interesting) film you've seen this year?
4. Who is .... (popular) singer in your country?
5. Who is .... (young) in your family?
6. Who is .... (old) in your family?
7. Who is .... (tall) in your class?
8. Who is .... (clever) in your class?

10 Reader's Corner

1 What's Your Travel Personality? Do the quiz and find out.

Quiz

1. You prefer to be
   A outdoors.
   B in a café or restaurant.
   C at a spa.

2. You like to watch
   A National Geographic Explorer.
   B The Food Network.
   C Lifestyles of the Rich and Famous.

3. On your day off, you like to
   A discover new places.
   B enjoy a good meal.
   C relax.

4. You usually read
   A adventure stories.
   B cookery books.
   C glossy magazines.

5. You feel most comfortable in
   A trainers.
   B an apron.
   C pyjamas.

Mostly A answers:

The Adventurer

You love sport and adventure and like a lot of action in your life. You like the kind of holiday where there's plenty to do and lots of places to explore.

Mostly B answers:

The Gourmet

You love anything that involves cooking or eating. You like the type of holiday where there are lots of restaurants and cafés to choose from.

Mostly C answers:

The Pampered One

You like to live in luxury and enjoy peace and quiet. You like the type of holiday where you don't have to do anything but lie on the beach all day.

2 Read the key again and match the holiday destinations to the travel personalities.

1 The Adventurer   A A week in a five-star hotel in Paris.
2 The Gourmet   B A Safari holiday in Kenya.
3 The Pampered One   C A week on a Caribbean island.

3 Now that you know your travel personality, talk to your partner about it. Mention some of the places you would like to visit.

Progress Check

Vocabulary & Grammar

A Circle the correct item.

1 Is it OK to drink the .... water?
   A tip   B tap   C bottle

2 The Victoria .... are in Africa.
   A Caves   B Falls   C Beaches

3 Look at the sign! You .... switch off your mobile phone.
   A must   B can   C can't

4 Brazil is .... country I've ever visited.
   A beautiful   B more beautiful
   C the most beautiful

5 He lived in Venezuela .... two years.
   A since   B for   C already

6 I .... a song competition last year.
   A won   B has won   C win

7 A .... is someone who shows tourists around places such as museums or cities.
   A chef   B tour guide
   C vet

8 The Black .... is in Germany.
   A River   B Lake   C Forest

9 He hasn't picked up the tickets ....
   A never   B yet   C ever

10 The Johnsons moved .... yesterday.
   A jobs   B home   C house

11 You .... take pets on board. It's not allowed!
   A mustn't   B must   C can

12 10 is an .... number.
   A unlucky   B even   C odd

13 Melanie is the thinnest girl .... the class.
   A of   B at   C in

14 Do you like to travel ....?
   A bright   B light   C alright

15 Bob is the .... student in our class.
   A lazy   B lazier   C laziest

16 .... to Julie's party last night?
   A Did you go   B Do you go
   C Have you gone

17 You should keep your money in the hotel ....
   A safe   B pool   C carrier

18 I've .... been to Egypt in my life!
   A ever   B yet   C never

19 Hello, Chris. .... seeing you here!
   A Fancy   B Like   C Love

20 I think the .... exciting book I've ever read is "Robinson Crusoe".
   A very   B more   C most

Communication

B Complete the exchanges.

a It's kind of you to say so!
b It's nice that you've noticed!
c You look great!
d Thank you, sir!
e You look fantastic in that dress!

1 A: ....
   B: Thanks! I've lost a bit of weight recently.

2 A: Your hair looks lovely!
   B: ....

3 A: ....
   B: Thanks! You've made my day!

4 A: You're the best cook I've ever known!
   B: ....

5 A: You're an excellent student, Stuart!
   B: ....

(Total: ——— 25x4   100 marks)

85

Irregular Verbs

Infinitive	Past	Past Participle	Infinitive	Past	Past Participle
be	was	been	lie	lay	lain
bear	bore	born(e)	light	lit	lit
beat	beat	beaten	lose	lost	lost
become	became	become	make	made	made
begin	began	begun	mean	meant	meant
bite	bit	bitten	meet	met	met
blow	blew	blown	pay	paid	paid
break	broke	broken	put	put	put
bring	brought	brought	read	read	read
build	built	built	ride	rode	ridden
burn	burnt (burned)	burnt (burned)	ring	rang	rung
burst	burst	burst	rise	rose	risen
buy	bought	bought	run	ran	run
can	could	(been able to)	say	said	said
catch	caught	caught	see	saw	seen
choose	chose	chosen	seek	sought	sought
come	came	come	sell	sold	sold
cost	cost	cost	send	sent	sent
cut	cut	cut	set	set	set
deal	dealt	dealt	sew	sewed	sewn
dig	dug	dug	shake	shook	shaken
do	did	done	shine	shone	shone
dream	dreamt (dreamed)	dreamt (dreamed)	shoot	shot	shot
drink	drank	drunk	show	showed	shown
drive	drove	driven	shut	shut	shut
eat	ate	eaten	sing	sang	sung
fall	fell	fallen	sit	sat	sat
feed	fed	fed	sleep	slept	slept
feel	felt	felt	smell	smelt (smelled)	smelt (smelled)
fight	fought	fought	speak	spoke	spoken
find	found	found	spell	spelt (spelled)	spelt (spelled)
flee	fled	fled	spend	spent	spent
fly	flew	flown	split	split	split
forbid	forbade	forbidden	spread	spread	spread
forget	forgot	forgotten	spring	sprang	sprung
forgive	forgave	forgiven	stand	stood	stood
freeze	froze	frozen	steal	stole	stolen
get	got	got	stick	stuck	stuck
give	gave	given	sting	stung	stung
go	went	gone	stink	stank	stunk
grow	grew	grown	strike	struck	struck
hang	hung (hanged)	hung (hanged)	swear	swore	sworn
have	had	had	sweep	swept	swept
hear	heard	heard	swim	swam	swum
hide	hid	hidden	take	took	taken
hit	hit	hit	teach	taught	taught
hold	held	held	tear	tore	torn
hurt	hurt	hurt	tell	told	told
keep	kept	kept	think	thought	thought
know	knew	known	throw	threw	thrown
lay	laid	laid	understand	understood	understood
lead	led	led	wake	woke	woken
learn	learnt (learned)	learnt (learned)	wear	wore	worn
leave	left	left	win	won	won
lend	lent	lent	write	wrote	written
let	let	let			